Tourism and Poverty Reduction

Pathways to Prosperity

Jonathan Mitchell and Caroline Ashley

Overseas Development
Institute

earthscan

publishing for a sustainable future

London • Sterling, VA

First published by Earthscan in the UK and US in 2010

HB ISBN: 978-1-84407-888-2
PB ISBN: 978-1-84407-889-9

Typeset by JS Typesetting Ltd, Porthcawl, Mid Glamorgan
Cover design by Yvonne Booth

Overseas Development Institute
111 Westminster Bridge Road
London SE1 7JD

For a full list of publications please contact:

Earthscan
Dunstan House
14a St Cross Street
London EC1N 8XA, UK
Tel: +44 (0)20 7841 1930
Fax: +44 (0)20 7242 1474
Email: earthinfo@earthscan.co.uk
Web: **www.earthscan.co.uk**

22883 Quicksilver Drive, Sterling, VA 20166-2012, US

Earthscan publishes in association with the International Institute for Environment and
Development

A catalogue record for this book is available from the British Library

Library of Congress Cataloging-in-Publication Data
Mitchell, Jonathan.
    Tourism and Poverty reduction : pathways to prosperity / Jonathan Mitchell and Caroline
Ashley.
      p. cm.
    Includes bibliographical references and index.
    ISBN 978-1-84407-888-2 (hardback) – ISBN 978-1-84407-889-9 (pbk.) 1. Tourism.
2. Tourism–Government policy. 3. Poverty–Government policy. I. Ashley, Caroline. II. Title.
    G155.A1M54 2010
    338.4'791–dc22

                                                                           2009033073

This book was printed in the UK by
The Cromwell Press Group. The paper
used is FSC certified.

Mixed Sources
Product group from well-managed
forests and other controlled sources
www.fsc.org Cert no. TT-COC-2082
© 1996 Forest Stewardship Council

Contents

List of Figures, Tables and Boxes

Figures

Tables

Boxes

Acknowledgements

Many people have helped us to write this book. Most important are our families who encouraged us to be curious about the world as kids – and have then tolerated the consequences of this curiosity into adulthood.

The idea that tourism can benefit the poor germinated during our experiences living in southern Africa during the euphoric democratic transformations there in the 1990s – as the newly enfranchised majority tried to engage productively with the historically 'white'-owned tourism industry for the first time.

We then refined our thinking at the Overseas Development Institute (ODI) in London, testing our ideas in many different countries. We have benefited from the support of organizations such as the Netherlands Development Organization (SNV), the World Bank and the International Finance Corporation (IFC), several agencies of the United Nations and the out-bound tourist industry in the financing of this work and giving us the space to refine our approach.

This book has its origins in a literature review on tourism and poverty reduction for the World Bank in 2007. We acknowledge the support of the World Bank and the Bank-Netherlands Partnership Program in funding this study, and colleagues from the World Bank for sharing information and ideas in a great example of technical collaboration with ODI. The engagement with Shaun Mann, Louise Fox, Alan Gelb and others has strongly influenced us.

Within ODI, the authors gratefully acknowledge the research input of Yiran Wei, Andresa Lagerborg, Pamela Muckosy, Gemma Jones, Vinzenzo Salerno, Dirk-Willem te Velde, Massimiliano Cali and Stephanie Levy, and Macclesfield's own Jenny Laidlaw in particular. The detailed comments of four leading members of the tourism and development research field – Harold Goodwin, Martin Mowforth, David Harrison and Adam Blake – were really helpful in the revision of the manuscript.

The findings, interpretations and conclusions in this volume do not necessarily represent the views of the Executive Directors of the World Bank or of anyone else other than the authors.

List of Acronyms and Abbreviations

CBT	community-based tourism
CCA	Conservation Corporation Africa
CGE	Computable General Equilibrium
CSR	corporate social responsibility
DFID	Department for International Development
DTIS	Diagnostic Trade Intervention Studies
EOR	employment:output ratio
FTO	Federation of Tour Operators
GDP	gross domestic product
GTZ	German international cooperation enterprise for sustainable development
ICRT	International Centre for Responsible Tourism
IFC	International Finance Corporation
IICA	Inter-American Institute for Cooperation on Agriculture
IIED	International Institute for Environment and Development
ILO	International Labour Organization
I–O	input–output
ISIC	International Standard Industrial Classification(s)
ITC	International Trade Centre
LDCs	Least Developed Countries
MDG	Millennium Development Goal
MSE	micro and small enterprise
NGOs	non-governmental organizations
ODI	Overseas Development Institute
OE	Oxford Economics
OECD	Organisation for Economic Co-operation and Development
PPT	pro-poor tourism
SAMs	Social Accounting Matrices
SLA	sustainable livelihoods analysis
SME	small and medium enterprise
SMME	small, medium and micro enterprise
SNA	United Nations System of National Accounts
SNV	the Netherlands development organization

ST-EP	Sustainable Tourism – Eliminating Poverty
SWOT	strengths, weaknesses, opportunities, threats
TSA	Tourism Satellite Account
UNDP	United Nations Development Programme
UNWTO	United Nations World Tourism Organization
VCA	value chain analysis
WEF	World Economic Forum
WTO	World Tourism Organization
WTTC	World Travel and Tourism Council

1
Introduction

In 2008, 924 million tourists travelled abroad. That is a lot of people – amounting to over 100,000 people every hour. Three-quarters of these journeys started in a high or upper-middle income country. Remarkably 40 per cent of these journeys ended in a developing country destination. International tourists are significantly better than development agencies at spending money in poor countries. In 2007 tourists spent US$295 billion in developing countries – almost three times the level of official development assistance. It is for this reason that tourism has been described as the world's largest voluntary transfer of resources from rich people to poor people. Understanding the impact on poor countries of this huge inflow of well-heeled humanity has fascinated researchers since mainstream tourism started in the 1970s.

Despite the voluminous research outputs of economists, anthropologists, sociologists, geographers and a range of development practitioners, there is little understanding and no consensus on what impact tourism has had on poverty in the developing world.

The aims of this book are to gather together what is already known about the poverty-reducing impacts of tourism across a range of developing countries to answer three questions:

1 What are the pathways by which tourism affects the poor?
2 What is the evidence of the effects of each of these pathways?
3 How can these pathways be measured?

The goal of this book is both practical and urgent – to understand whether a private sector service activity, like tourism, can reduce poverty in developing countries. The lessons emerging from this review are intended to be useful and relevant. We hope this book is used by researchers and students, but also by development practitioners, public policy makers, civil society organizations and those living around and working in the tourist industry.

Our focus is on the economic effects of tourism on destinations. A broad range of economic effects are examined: direct and indirect; financial and non-financial; static and dynamic. While recognizing that the non-economic impacts of tourism can be important to those living in destinations, the rationale for this focus on economic effects is threefold.

First, there already exists a huge amount of literature focusing on the anthropological, social and environmental impacts of tourism. Research examining the economic effects of tourism on poor people is more limited and, hence, is in greater needs.

Second, the economics literature examining the link between tourism and poverty – such that exists – is a broad church. Findings are scattered across a range of approaches using different research methods and scales of analysis that are developing in splendid, and almost total, isolation from each other. The content and bibliographies of studies on tourism and poverty raise the question of whether many researchers are even aware of the existence of relevant work on the same issue emanating from different stables.

This book has discovered pockets of excellent and relevant scholarship, existing across a broad range of approaches, but with precious little effort to build bridges between these islands of expertise. We face the paradox that the increasing variety provided by greater research specialization has sometimes allowed us to become more, not less, parochial. As with popular music, greater variety has not always delivered greater choice. This book is about synthesis – not just because we all benefit from sharing ideas but because, in doing so, we test and sharpen our own thoughts. 'Talking Timbukto' is not a magical album just because the late Ali Farka Toure and Ry Cooder are superb individual musicians; it is because they blended Malian and American blues to create something truly special. This book represents an attempt figuratively to climb a tree to get a broader view of the research landscape and bring these disparate threads of research together.

Third, focusing on the economic effects of tourism on the poor goes to the heart of what is currently the most critical challenge facing development. The first Millennium Development Goal (MDG) – halving the 1995 rate of US$1-a-day poverty by 2015 – is a promise made at the dawn of the new millennium by global leadership. Partly influenced by the impact on poverty of buoyant growth in Asia and partly by the failure of many social welfare-orientated development programmes to reduce poverty, the focus on how to achieve the first MDG is narrowing. Stimulating an inclusive pattern of dynamic economic growth in developing countries, especially in Africa, is increasingly identified as the central challenge to successfully meeting the MDG targets.

Because relevant academic literature in this field is not abundant – and often not particularly policy relevant or empirically based – a book restricting itself to this type of research would be frustratingly short and inconclusive. To avoid this, we have drawn heavily on the so-called 'grey' literature. This is because much of the most relevant research, which has been written for policy makers by practitioners with an interest in poverty impacts, has not been through a formal peer review process. The reader must be as vigilant as the authors in recognizing that we are often dealing with a literature of variable quality, and so have a responsibility to retain a healthy scepticism about claims made without an adequate foundation.

This book focuses on Africa because this continent presents people working in development – and poor people themselves – with the most intractable contemporary development challenge. However, we include work from Asia and Latin America. This partly reflects the global shortage of sound analysis available, so putting up geographic barriers to the use of the limited supply of good work around makes little sense. Also, as illustrated later in this book, whilst tourism has shown impressive rates of growth in parts of Africa, the density of poverty-reducing local linkages is variable. Other places, particularly some parts of Asia, show a different pattern with much stronger links between tourism and poor people in the destination economy. In this sense, limiting our study to Africa simply illustrates the problem – to demonstrate solutions we need to look more broadly.

In the same way that there are different types of poverty, there are also different types of tourism. In this book we have tried to explicitly distinguish between different segments of the tourism market – where material allows. In parts of Africa, mainstream beach tourism and business tourism are more important than the traditional preoccupation with low volume wildlife-related tourism. The rationale for seeking a rich mix of tourism forms is that different types of tourism can have different impacts on the poor – and these differences are important for policy makers. However, the extent to which the existing literature differentiates by segments of the tourist market is generally disappointing.

Statements about the impact of tourism on the poor should also be qualified in terms of which of the resource 'poor' are affected. The literature is often not very rigorous in applying terms like 'poor' people, 'local' people, 'unskilled' and 'semi-skilled' labour. Local area studies usually implicitly focus on poor households within a destination, and not on poor households elsewhere. The distinction between effects of tourism on poor households within, and outside, tourist destinations often explains why studies at contrasting spatial scales of analysis have different conclusions about the effect of tourism on the poor – they look at different groups of people. In this book we highlight distinctions such as these, where answers to questions about how tourism affects poverty may reflect the research methods used as much as the performance of this sector of the economy.

This book is split into three sections. The first section provides an introduction to the issues covered. In the second section, evidence from the literature about the different pathways leading from tourism to the poor is reviewed. In the third section a critical assessment of the rich variety of tools that researchers have used to measure the effects of tourism on poverty is outlined.

Current debates, policy questions and the lack of data

There are diverse views on the effects of tourism on developing country destinations and the populations within them.

At the multilateral level, the United Nations World Tourism Organization (UNWTO) (previously the World Tourism Organization or WTO) is a sector advocacy organization that has been a firm proponent of tourism's contribution to poverty reduction (WTO, 2001, 2002a). Since 2002 it has specifically recommended the adoption of pro-poor approaches (WTO, 2002b, 2004). The UNWTO New Year message for 2007 stated that this year:

> ...should be a year to consolidate tourism as a key agent in the fight against poverty and a primary tool for sustainable development (UNWTO, 2007).

Many national governments in developing countries have recent and explicit policy statements asserting a role for tourism in strategies for the reduction of poverty. About 80 per cent of African Poverty Reduction Strategy Papers include a reference to encouraging tourism (Gerosa, 2003). Although tourism advocates often leap on this as evidence that African governments understand the potentially positive role of tourism, the priority afforded to tourism in important policy documents is very much less than more traditional preoccupations with agriculture, rural development and infrastructure.

At a local level many local governments, non-governmental organizations (NGOs) and civil society organizations embrace tourism as a tool to facilitate local economic development. However, the empirical basis for making policy choices or recommendations often appears thin, as Box 1.1 illustrates.

There are others who see the pro-poor potential of tourism as over-stated. Tourism is criticized by some as having high 'leakages', benefiting only a skilled labour 'aristocracy' and representing an unacceptable juxtaposition between the luxury enjoyed by the tourist and the poor living conditions for people situated around the destinations (see Table 1.1). Many Western tourism researchers have highlighted the negative cultural and social effects of tourism on poor local communities and frequently question the supposed economic benefits of trade in tourism services (Diamond, 1977; Broham, 1996; Clancy, 2001; Scheyvens, 2002; Jules, 2005; Slob and Wilde-Ramsing, 2006; UNEP, 2007).

A serious problem confronting organizations that are either euphoric or despondent about the destination effects of tourism is the often worryingly weak empirical basis for their assertions. Strong views seem to be strongly held, often without the burden of credible evidence. Even where data are cited, the analysis is often unable to withstand rigorous scrutiny. Examples of this are the oft-repeated figures about the level of leakages of tourist revenue, dissected further in Chapter 5.

Developing country governments and donors alike are preoccupied with the imperative to allocate scarce investment funds wisely to make optimal use of national assets and maximize sustainable poverty reduction and shared economic growth. Policy makers need information about the extent to which investment in tourism will facilitate meeting their poverty reduction objectives. They need to know how an expansion of tourism demand can affect poverty

Box 1.1 *Support for pro-poor tourism strategies but not measuring impacts*

Harold Goodwin (2006a) observes:

> *In the last ten years, despite the increasing focus on tourism and poverty reduction, there have been very few reported interventions where any attempt has been made to measure beneficiary impact. With major programmes of intervention underway through SNV and ST-EP there is a pressing need to begin to measure and report impacts.*

Sadly, this assertion from one of the leading thinkers in pro-poor tourism (PPT) has much to support it.

The WTO launched its publication *Tourism and Poverty Alleviation* in Johannesburg in 2002 (WTO, 2002b); published recommendations for action on tourism and poverty alleviation in 2004 (WTO, 2004); and has launched a Foundation: Sustainable Tourism – Eliminating Poverty (ST-EP) that is now developing pilot projects in many developing countries. All this is based on the assumption that tourism can be an effective tool for poverty reduction. The WTO called for broad and specific indicators of poverty alleviation resulting from tourism, saying that 'such reporting may be a condition of any assistance given' (WTO, 2004). However, to date, WTO and ST-EP are not generating the empirical evidence that would either provide the information for their partners to overhaul tourism policy in a pro-poor way, or would substantiate the benefits of specific interventions.

The bulk of the pro-poor tourism literature has not been aimed at measuring impact but on assessing what strategies can help expand impacts on the poor. While there have been practical reasons to focus on promoting interventions, the lack of quantification of impact is indeed recognized as a weakness in the pro-poor tourism literature by its proponents (Saville, 2001; Poultney and Spenceley, 2001; Nicanor, 2001; Bah and Goodwin, 2003; PPT Partnership, 2004; McNab, 2005; Ashley et al, 2005; Goodwin, 2006a) as well as its detractors (Chok and Macbeth, 2007).

Tourism advisers from the Netherlands Development Organization, SNV, have just completed an assessment of government strategies for increasing local economic impacts of tourism in Rwanda, Kenya, Ethiopia, Tanzania and Mozambique. Not only the assessments, but the policy document and strategies they review, are strikingly devoid of empirical evidence concerning impacts of tourism on poor people, bar some headline employment figures, a couple of pieces of data from village projects and the occasional statistic from a World Bank report (Verdugo, 2007; Weru, 2007; Mtui, 2007; Sarmento, 2007). Policy recommendations have fragile empirical foundations.

Table 1.1 *Examples of claims made by tourism researchers and practitioners*

Negative claims	Positive claims
Up to 85% of the supposed benefits of tourism 'leak' out of developing countries (cited in Bolwell and Weinz, 2008), due to the power of international tour operators (Broham, 1996), foreign ownership, and high import propensity of tourism (Jules, 2005)	Services generally, and tourism in particular, are among the most viable growth paths for developing countries due to relatively low entry barriers and buoyant growth (Benavides and Perez-Ducy, 2001)
Tourism employment is seasonal, low-paying and exploitative (Clancy, 2001; Slob and Wilde-Ramsing, 2006)	Although we need to be cautious of generalizations, 'tourism-led growth' is a reality and the sector often outpaces the manufacturing and agricultural sectors in its relative contribution to economic growth (Lejárraga and Walkenhorst, 2006)
Tourism employment is secured by those with skills, and is not accessible to the poor (Dwyer et al, 2000)	Compared with other sectors, a relatively high share of tourism employment is unskilled or semi-skilled and available to a wider cross-section of the labour market
Poor people are particularly vulnerable to the costs of tourism – wildlife damage to agriculture, opportunity costs of land, lost access to and depletion of natural resources	Tourism creates opportunities for peripherally located markets because the customer comes to the product (the tourist destination or excursion) and makes discretionary expenditure
Tourism expansion crowds out other domestic sectors, leading to de-industrialization and long-term reductions in welfare for the population (Dwyer et al, 2000; Chao et al, 2006)	Tourism has become one of the major sources of GDP growth in many of the Least Developed Countries and a key contributing factor for those that have graduated out of LDC status (Encontre, 2001)

compared, for instance, with another sector. The issue of how government policy can influence the poverty impacts of tourism is of particular concern.

Whilst this book cannot answer all these questions, it provides a start. The review outlines the conceptual links between tourism and poor people. It assembles evidence of the scale of these pathways and highlights some of the variables that appear to affect the strength of these relationships. It also helps in understanding where gaps exist and which gaps should be filled in order to be able to provide policy makers with the sound advice they currently lack.

Why focus on the tourism sector?

At first sight a focus on tourism from people driven by a desire to reduce world poverty seems incongruous. Can you really contribute to fighting poverty from a sun bed by the pool side? For poverty practitioners, tourism has three great attractions.

First, tourism is an important part of the economy in poor countries. Although aggregate tourism receipts[1] are concentrated in rich countries, like economic activity more generally, tourism is relatively more important in poorer counties than in rich countries (see Figure 1.1). Tourism is as significant as manufacturing, and much more important than mining, in the export basket of the Least Developed Countries (LDCs). The continent of Africa's share of global tourism (some 50.5 million arrivals in 2006 or 6 per cent of global arrivals of 851 million) is much larger than its average share of world trade. There are many poor countries, such as Ethiopia and The Gambia, which are small destinations in international terms, but for whom tourism makes an important contribution to the economy of 29.8 per cent and 33.1 per cent of total exports respectively (World Bank, 2009).

Secondly, long-term prospects for growth appear relatively robust, with developing countries capturing a growing share of the tourism market (Lejárraga and Walkenhorst, 2006). Trade in tourist services is the only economic sector where the South has consistently enjoyed a large trade surplus with the North.

The traditional panacea of export-led manufacturing as the answer for Africa still has its advocates (Teal, 2005). However, there is a growing recognition that the emergence of large, low income, predominantly Asian exporters of manufactured goods is fundamentally changing the world economy. Specifically, it is much less likely that Africans can productively engage with the world economy predominantly through the export of manufactured goods. This suggests that an economic transition from agriculture to service activities (such as tourism) – leapfrogging the manufacturing sector – may not be as fanciful as it would have sounded a few years ago.

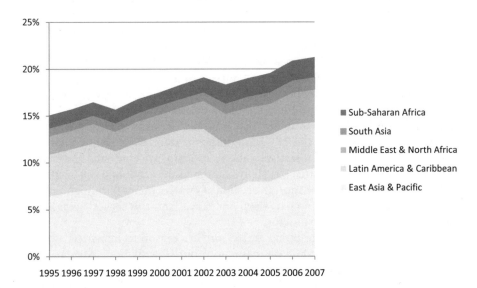

Figure 1.1 *International tourism receipts as a percentage of the world total, 1995–2007*

The third part of the case for poverty practitioners looking at tourism is the simplest. Under certain conditions, tourism can demonstrably benefit poor people. Furthermore, a number of strategies can boost these benefits to the poor, thus warranting policy attention so as not to fritter away this potential (DFID, 1999; Ashley et al, 2001; Ashley, 2006b; Mann, 2006).

Definitions

An important lesson emerging from this book is that definitions of basic terms vary. These differences have important impacts on the findings and impair meaningful comparisons. Researchers define terms differently, while economists and pro-poor tourism practitioners may use the same word with a quite different meaning. The analytical part of this exercise has been bedevilled by contrasting and often sloppy usage of terms found in the literature reviewed.

To illustrate the point, the contrasting definitions of 'tourism', 'pro-poor', and 'poor' are highlighted below. It is important to keep these definitional issues in mind when reviewing literature on the effects of tourism on poor people.

Tourism is defined as, 'the activities of people travelling to and staying in places outside their usual environment for no more than one year for leisure, business, and other purposes not related to an activity remunerated from the place visited' (World Bank, 2009, p393). While this definition of a 'tourist' is readily adopted by most, it is often quite tricky to apply in practice in a developing country. For instance, a lot of domestic tourism in developing countries – often very much under the radar of official statistics that will equate 'tourist' with 'foreigner' – is business tourism. A trader from a peripheral town who comes to the capital city to buy goods to take home to sell is a business tourist. However, if she sells any goods in the capital city, she is earning funds from the destination and becomes a migrant worker. The distinction is subtle and the implications of defining a person as a 'tourist' or a 'migrant' are important.

Defining the 'tourism sector' or 'tourism industry' itself, is also surprisingly difficult. This is partly because tourism is an economic activity which is a composite of services and goods surrounded by rather unclear boundaries – so it is inherently a slippery animal. Also 'tourism' is not a clearly identifiable sector of the economy in the 1993 international standard system of national accounts (SNA) – so official statistics about 'tourism' are contested. Activity in the sector is usually estimated simply by summing the economic sub-sectors of hotels, restaurants and transportation. But of course, many (although not all) tourists do rather more than eat, sleep and travel and this 'other' spending is not attributed to the tourist sector.

Recreation, culture, shopping and leisure are central to many tourism experiences. Sometimes spending on these 'non-tourist' activities is very significant and results in a lot of expenditure by tourists falling outside these tightly drawn International Standard Industrial Classification (ISIC) categories that constitute 'tourism' (see Box 1.2). Definitions of 'tourism' have, themselves, stimulated important debates within the literature reviewed.

Box 1.2 *The challenge of defining tourism: Narrow or broad, supply- or demand-led?*

The SNA is based on ISIC categories. This is a United Nations system for classifying economic data – by chopping the economy up into categories according to clear definitions. 'Tourism' is generally estimated by combining ISIC Division 55 (hotels and restaurants) with ISIC Divisions 60, 61, 62 and 63 (comprising land, water and air transport, and supporting transport activities respectively) (Slob and Wilde-Ramsing, 2006). Using this sector-based, supply-side definition, much tourist spending falls outside the official definition of 'tourism'.

To address this weakness, Tourism Satellite Accounts (TSAs) seek to define a larger and more realistic tourist sector by combining a demand-based definition (i.e. mainly what visitors spend their money on) with a supply-focused definition (keeping sectors as the basis for assessment).

Tourism demand is estimated mainly as resulting from tourist expenditure but also other elements of demand such as capital formation (WTO, 2000). This demand is then related to different sectors of the economy, to identify industries that are 'tourism characteristic' (industries that would cease without tourist consumption) and 'tourism connected' (industries where tourists consume significant quantities of the output) (Medlik, 2003, p96). These in turn are used to assess the size of a broadly defined tourism economy. Two different terms are important:

1   Gross domestic product (GDP) of tourism industries is the total value added by all 'tourism characteristic' industries, including the share of their output that is sold to non-tourists. This supply-based definition is useful for maintaining compatibility with SNA and for comparison with other sectors.
2   Tourism GDP is the value added specifically due to tourism expenditure across all economic sectors, whether they are 'tourism characteristic' or not. This demand-based definition is a more accurate reflection of activity caused by tourists.

Another important distinction, emphasized by the World Travel and Tourism Council (WTTC) (WTTC and OE, 2006) is between the 'travel and tourism industry' and the 'travel and tourism economy'. Estimates of the size of the travel and tourism industry are derived only from tourism consumption. Estimates of the size of the larger travel and tourism economy derive from 'total tourism demand' which – in addition to tourism consumption – also includes government spending, capital formation, and travel and tourism non-visitor exports. This calculation includes indirect value added from sectors that supply the tourism sector.

The emergence of TSAs is largely a counter-reaction to the tight definitions of the official tourism sector. Input-output tables are used to build up a broader view of the tourist economy by measuring the scale of inter-sector linkages between narrowly defined 'tourism' and the rest of the economy. The results generated by applying these tools suggest that definitional issues are not just the territory of pedants. Often the 'true' size of the tourism economy is found to be at least twice as large as that reflected in the official estimates derived from the accommodation, restaurant and travel sectors in the national accounts.

It may seem self-evident that policy questions about how tourism contributes to poverty reduction are about achieving pro-poor growth from tourism. However, this stimulates definitional debates because 'pro-poor growth' is itself a contested term.

There is an undemanding definition of pro-poor growth (growth where any positive benefit at all that trickles down to the poor is regarded as 'pro-poor'). By this definition almost all economic growth is pro-poor – even if the main beneficiaries of growth are the non-poor and growth is associated with rising inequality. At the other end of the spectrum is a restrictive definition of 'pro-poor' growth (that growth is only pro-poor if it reduces inequality) under which most commercial growth – certainly in tourism – would be excluded (see Box 1.3). Neither is it particularly helpful in guiding policy approaches towards tourism.

Whilst the idea of finding a pattern of growth which is redistributive is obviously appealing to many development specialists, the restrictive definition creates real difficulties in practical application. For instance, the most dramatic reduction in poverty ever experienced in world history (the graduation of about 800 million Chinese out of poverty during the decade after 1995) would not be defined as pro-poor growth because this rapid decline in poverty was associated with increasing inequality, albeit from very low levels. Also, during a period of negative growth, the restrictive definition would regard a period where the living standards of the poor were falling more slowly than the welfare of the rich as 'pro-poor'. Even though poverty is increasing, inequality is reducing – hardly a desirable outcome developmentally.

The pro-poor growth debates also include some interesting discussion in the middle ground (Grinspun, 2004; Osmani, 2005). Applying the concept of incremental benefits implies that pro-poor tourism is tourism that boosts the net benefits to the poor in comparison to what they would otherwise have been. This definition has conceptual problems but is more oriented to the policy priority to reduce poverty and tallies with common usage of the term 'pro-poor tourism'.

However, agonizing over subtle nuances in which definition of pro-poor tourism to adopt is not the best use of our time. Of concern to policy makers and practitioners in the field is not so much how to label their tourism, but how – and how much – to invest in developing tourism; the likely impact on poverty; and how to enhance the poverty reduction effect. This pragmatic approach represents an implicit acceptance of Osmani's relative definition (2005) – growth is pro-poor if it benefits the resource poor more than in the past.

Box 1.3 *Applying definitions of pro-poor growth to tourism*

The broad definition of pro-poor growth (summarized in Ravallion, 2004) labels growth as pro-poor so long as the poor benefit (i.e. absolute or relative poverty falls, even if inequality increases). Most episodes of growth would therefore fall under this so-called World Bank definition of pro-poor growth. Applied to the tourism sector this would require that net benefits to the poor are positive. In practice this would be difficult to assess, as positive flows tend to be financial and evident, while the negative effects of tourism are more often non-financial impacts on livelihoods (access to resources) or even more intangible assets such as culture. In terms of policy usage, this broad definition may lead a few to recognize the need to assess the negatives, but would probably lead many more to simply reassure themselves that tourism growth is inherently pro-poor.

The narrow definition of pro-poor growth (expounded by Kakwani and Pernia, 2000) requires that the poor benefit proportionately more than others, so that inequality is reduced along with poverty. In other words, tourism is only pro-poor if it reduces inequality as well as directing resources to poor people. Although the authors have found some examples of supply chains into the tourism value chain that may meet this restrictive definition of pro-poor tourism, they are few and far between. In fact, much developing country government public expenditure fails to be redistributive in this sense. Tourism is a private sector-driven activity and needs to generate returns to the owners of businesses in order to be sustainable. There can be few commercial activities that successfully meet this benchmark of pro-poor growth.

The policy implications of defining most tourism (indeed most private sector development) as anti-poor are questionable. This is a poor rationale for not developing the tourism industry if it can generate substantial net benefits for poor people that exceed their opportunity costs (what they would be doing if there was no tourism) – particularly if these net benefits can be increased via the type of deliberate interventions highlighted in this review. This thought is echoed in criticisms of both the narrow and wide definitions.

Osmani (2005, p1) argues that 'pro-poor growth demands a break with the past that makes growth more conducive to poverty reduction... from the point of view of the poor; there must be an improvement over business as usual'. So 'pro-poor' growth is simply growth that benefits the poor more than some previous benchmark. In practical terms, this moves us away from categorizing whether a growth experience is or is not pro-poor, and focuses minds on both enhancing poverty impacts and comparing whether a particular set of policies is likely to be more pro-poor than another. This emphasis on boosting net benefits is embraced by the definition of pro-poor tourism posted by the Pro-Poor Tourism Partnership (PPT Partnership), which first coined the phrase (PPT Partnership, no date). This need to shift emphasis from the conceptual to the practical is also recognized by Ravallion (2004, p1), who argues, 'the real issue is not whether growth is pro-poor but how pro-poor it is'.

Defining how tourism affects 'the poor' and 'poverty reduction' is futile without defining who the 'poor' are and what is meant by poverty reduction. And yet, in the wide-ranging tourism studies literature, this is generally attempted in only a rather crude way. Documents reviewed often do not address the issue directly and implicitly assume that, for instance, tourism growth inevitably benefits the poor – an echo of the undemanding definition of pro-poor growth. Alternatively, studies focus on specific groups of people who may act as proxies for the poor (for instance 'rural residents' or 'crafters'). This lack of careful definition is a weakness in the application of pro-poor tourism (Jamieson et al, 2004).

There are three key difficulties in seeking to apply the conventional international income poverty benchmark of extreme poverty (US$1 per person per day at 1995 purchasing power parity). The first is a practical one. Virtually no tourism studies apply this international ruler to measure the impact of the tourist sector. The second difficulty is that many developing countries apply national income poverty rates that are much lower than the international 'dollar a day' formulation. The third difficulty is that poverty itself is now widely regarded as a multi-dimensional phenomenon. The ability of the poor to influence decisions that affect their lives, vulnerability or resilience to shocks, access to services and assets, strength or disruption of social networks, are all important factors to take into account in assessing poverty.[2] Tourism may affect many of these aspects of well-being or livelihoods, without directly changing household income (Gujadhur, 2001; Saville, 2001; Bramman and Fundación Acción Amazonia, 2001; Ashley and Jones, 2001; Poultney and Spenceley, 2001).

To avoid falling at this definitional hurdle, we will retain an agnostic view on what is the correct poverty level to apply to tourism studies and, instead, highlight the poverty line selected (if any) by researchers in the studies reviewed. The focus is on financial flows, but highlighting also the other impacts that affect livelihoods and economic aspects of well-being.

In our own work we are increasingly using a dynamic and self-categorizing definition of 'poverty'. For instance, asking hotel managers what proportion of their staff are from a poor background, as a way of estimating the role of tourism in lifting hotel employees out of poverty over time.

Types of literature available

This book straddles an extremely diverse and fragmented research literature (Zhao and Ritchie, 2007). Researchers in a rich mix of institutions have been assessing issues relevant to tourism and poverty. Different approaches have been adopted by researchers seeking to answer somewhat different questions for a variety of institutional, professional and philosophical reasons. Most have addressed rather specific pieces of the tourism and poverty jig-saw and, in so doing, become so specialized that they have lost the ability to talk to others outside the confines of their own disciplinary silo. Few have seen the importance of harnessing the insights provided by a range of different approaches to answer the question 'how can tourism reduce poverty?' This book is a quite deliberate attempt to break out of this rut and assess the contribution of a range of approaches to our question.

Some analyses aim to measure the contribution of tourism to the wider economy. This has been a particular focus of TSAs, which aim to demonstrate the size (and, therefore, importance) of tourism. Other analyses explore the impacts of a specific tourist enterprise or intervention. For example, researchers working with community-based tourism, eco-tourism, or corporate social responsibility have documented the direct impacts of tourism at the enterprise or very local area level, tending to overlook the more indirect ways that tourism can affect poverty.

A sensible way of categorizing this diverse literature is to group it in terms of what the researchers themselves are trying to achieve. The four categories of research methods in Table 1.2 address four quite distinct questions:

1 What are the economic effects of tourism on the rest of the economy?
2 How big is tourism?
3 In what ways does tourism affect poor people?
4 How can tourism be grown?

Assessing the effects of tourism activities on the economy

This has mainly been the domain of quantitative academic economists working in universities. They have used a range of economic tools to assess the economic impact of tourism. The results of this kind of analysis are reported in the academic literature, but with limited evidence of engagement with policy makers. These approaches look beyond the bald arrival numbers and aggregate spend statistics, to model how tourism affects wider and longer-term prospects for economic growth. Some recent analyses have looked at the impact of tourism on specific groups and how policy variables influence the results of who benefits from tourism.

Table 1.2 *A categorization of the literature*

Primary objective of analysis	Research methods used
Assess the economic effects (direct, indirect, static and dynamic) of tourism activities on the (macro) economy	Regression analysis, Social Accounting Matrices, Computable Generalized Equilibrium models
Describe the size of the tourist sector	Tourism Satellite Accounts
Measure impacts of tourism on poor people or local economies at tourist destinations	Livelihoods analysis, enterprise analysis, local economic mapping and pro-poor value chain analysis
Develop and enhance the tourism sector, its growth and competitiveness	Tourism master plans and conventional value chain analysis

Exploring the macro-economic trends, econometric models and cross-country regression analysis have been used to look for correspondence between tourism growth and other economic change over time. For example, studies have assessed the correspondence between tourism growth and variables such as income levels, volatility of GDP growth and competitiveness of non-tourism exports, and have explored such relationships for specific countries or groups of countries such as small island states (Ghali, 1976; Brau et al, 2003; Oh, 2005; Brakke, 2005; Algieri, 2006).

Another approach has been to build economic models for a specific destination economy, to assess impacts of tourism demand on other sectors and economic variables. Such models vary from relatively simple Input–Output models (I–O models) to Social Accounting Matrices (SAMs) and, more recently, Computable General Equilibrium models (CGE models) (Lin and Sung, 1984; Kweka et al, 2003; Aylward and Lutz, 2003; Bigsten and Shimeles, 2004; Sinclair et al, 2004; Kweka, 2004; Sahli and Nowak, 2005; Blake et al, 2008).

I–O models examine the links between a unit increase in tourism demand and resulting increases in demand for other sectors, so have traditionally been used to calculate 'tourism multipliers'. These much-used (and often misused) ratios describe the way the effects of changes in tourism demand ripple through the rest of the economy. SAMs can add a distributional element to such models by adding consideration of benefits that accrue to different types of households. Both I–O models and SAMs look only at one-off or static effects of a change in tourism demand. In contrast, CGEs are dynamic and designed to model the way that economies actually respond to changes in demand through price changes that lead to further changes in demand (Dwyer et al, 2000). CGEs are also well-suited to model the impact of policy changes. Although few analyses have been carried out in developing countries, the Nottingham Business School has illustrated the future potential of these approaches.

Estimating the size of the tourism sector

TSAs are a very significant contemporary focus for tourism research[3] and focus upon estimating the size of the tourism sector. They draw on input–output tables, combined with surveys of tourism spending, to assess the volume of economic activity related to tourism spending. TSAs seek to capture all the direct and indirect activity attributable to tourism. As a result, this tends to generate a larger estimate of the contribution of tourism to the economy than the SNA. Applying the logic that 'bigger is better', TSA results are used by lobbyists (private sector or ministries of tourism) to make the case that tourism is a more important economic sector than commonly regarded and, thus, deserves more favourable treatment from public-sector decision makers.

While the onerous data requirements for TSA are a particular burden for developing countries, there are now well over a dozen developing countries with TSAs. They are supported both by the UNWTO (which represents member governments) and the WTTC (the industry body), with slightly different methodological emphases.

Notwithstanding their popularity amongst industry lobbyists, TSAs shed little light on how different components of the tourism sector contribute to its aggregate impact, how those impacts are distributed and how they can be increased.

The Namibian TSA, published by WTTC (WTTC, 2006) provides an example. The 60-page document provides a very clear message that tourism makes an important economic contribution to Namibia. Nearly 20 graphs and tables comparing Namibian results with others in sub-Saharan Africa are used to reinforce the message that investment should be encouraged and growth rates maintained. But the extensive data that goes into building the supply side and demand side aggregates are not disaggregated to illustrate how economic impact, or indirect to direct ratios, vary by type of tourist or type of tourism, nor how changes in the structure of tourism would deliver different aggregate results.

Measuring the impact of tourism on poor people or local economies in tourist destinations

The fields of anthropology, sociology, community development, community based conservation, micro enterprise and, more recently, pro-poor tourism, sustainable livelihoods and corporate social responsibility (CSR), have spawned a host of a studies that focus on the impacts of tourism on specific groups of poor people in local areas. They are usually conducted by NGOs, researchers, community organizations, conservation organizations, consultants, students, or – increasingly – private sector operators. The purpose is generally to understand how to enhance impacts on the lives of a specific target group and to assist in evaluating or designing interventions. Or they may aim to highlight negative impacts of tourism and advocate for alternative development paths.

Most attempts to actually measure the effects of tourism on poor people have been focused at the micro level – a single enterprise (a lodge, resort, or community business), or related enterprises within a single community. There are innumerable such micro-level case studies (for example, Elliot, 1998; Elliot and Mwangi, 1998; Gujadhur, 2001; Bramman and Fundación Acción Amazonia, 2001; Halstead, 2003; Murphy and Halstead, 2003; Mulonga and Murphy, 2003; Clauzel, 2005; McNab, 2005; Hainsworth, 2006). The enterprises studied are often those that are not mainstream tourism products but are pro-poor in some way. Methods vary but usually use a combination of sustainable livelihoods analysis (SLA) (Ashley, 2000), which includes non-financial impacts on how people live, and micro-economic analysis of enterprise operations (revenues, profits, wages and so on). These studies focus heavily on how to boost shares of direct benefits to the poor, usually with little consideration of the wider growth of tourism, or other types of economic impacts.

Some of the most useful findings in recent years come from pro-poor analyses that adopt a somewhat broader lens. First, there are some studies that have focused not just on one tourism enterprise, but that compare pro-poor impact data across a cluster of enterprises. For example, studies of African safari lodges by MAFISA, a Johannesburg-based research organization (Massyn and Koch, 2004a, 2004b), or Caribbean resorts by GTZ, the German international cooperation enterprise for sustainable development, help to illustrate how key structural or operational factors affect pro-poor flows (Lengefeld and Beyer, 2006).

Second, pro-poor assessment has recently moved to mapping the entire tourism economy or value chain (a value chain covers all elements of providing goods and services to tourists, from supply of inputs to final consumption of goods and services, and includes analysis of the support institutions and governance issues within which these stakeholders operate) (Ashley 2006a; Mitchell and Faal, 2007; Mitchell and Le Chi, 2007). This approach is no longer bound to one pre-defined community but can ask the question, which poor people are most affected by engagement in this tourism industry? The aim of this work is to provide pro-poor guidance into wider policy on development of the sector. Because it analyses participation of the poor in the overall value chain, the studies can integrate questions about the shares of benefits accruing to the poor with other questions about returns to other stakeholders, how the overall chain is developing, and where priority areas to focus pro-poor interventions are.

Developing and enhancing the tourism sector, its growth and competitiveness

Probably the best-resourced area of tourism research is work that is done for developing tourism master plans – or variants thereof. Such plans are generally funded by governments and donors and undertaken by specialized Western tourism consultancy practices.

Tourism plans usually aim to set policy and budget priorities for tourism infrastructure, marketing, investment incentives and other public sector interventions that affect overall growth of the sector (CHL Consulting, 2002; Crompton and Christie, 2003; Hashemite Kingdom of Jordan, 2004; Government of the Federal Republic of Nigeria et al, 2006; FIAS, 2006; Fries et al, 2006). To do this they draw on analyses of tourism demand (segments, trends, expenditure and sometimes very comprehensive tourist surveys), and of the strength and weaknesses of their current tourism supply. Perhaps surprisingly, they rarely draw on research that investigates the distributional impact of tourism development, nor of 'what if...?' modelling of economic impacts of alternative proposed policy options.

Other types of research that aim to inform tourism sector development include value chain analysis (VCA) focused on sector competitiveness (such as FIAS, 2006 on Mozambique) and trade studies, such as Diagnostic Trade Intervention Studies (DTIS) initiated by UN organizations (see Sharma, 2005 on Tanzania; Mitchell and Faal, 2007 on The Gambia; Mitchell, 2008 on Cape Verde). Such studies look at obstacles to enhanced competitiveness, and are also aiming to inform ongoing policy of the government, though are not necessarily pegged to a specific master plan and may be as much about broad services or investment policy as about tourism.

In conclusion

There are several different ways of measuring and modelling the effects of changes in tourism demand on the broader economy – all of which are partial. In this diversity of approaches each has a different scope that reflects the contrasting interests of the tourism researcher. At heart, the key issue that should influence the choice of approach is 'what is the question you wish to answer?'

If the question is how can we grow the tourist sector or impress on decision makers in Treasury the real scale of existing tourism activities, TSAs or tourism master plans have an important role.

Academic economic analysis on the effects on the broader economy of changes in tourism demand has injected much-needed rigour into the debate, in the sense of helping us understand some of the reasons why tourism has particular effects on the macro-economy. These approaches also tend to analyse linkages between the tourist and non-tourist economies more systematically than others. However, most of the analysis has a limited focus on the impact of tourism on the poor and is often rather isolated from policy.

By contrast, most of the pro-poor tourism literature is so heavily focused on benefit shares accruing to specific poor groups it almost appears as if re-searchers believe the key function of tourism is to benefit poor people. Much pro-poor tourism research has ignored the health of the mainstream tourism sector itself and can be parochial in the sense of focusing on a beneficiary community and missing important impacts (particularly indirect, induced and dynamic impacts) through which tourism activity can significantly affect large numbers of poor people.

Table 1.3 lists the main methods used in these bodies of research, and sum-marizes the main research foci of each. Note the rather narrow focus of input–output analysis, tourism satellite accounts, master plans, conventional VCA and sustainable livelihoods approaches. From this analysis, the computable generated equilibrium modelling (incorporating social accounting matrices) and destination-level local economic mapping appear to have the broadest coverage of these important issues.

Notes

1 International tourism receipts are defined as 'expenditure of international inbound visitors including their payments to national carriers for international transport. They should also include any other prepayments made for goods/services received in the destination country' (Medlik, 2003, p96).

Table 1.3 *An overview of the research approaches in the literature*

Research focus \ Research methods	I-O analysis	TSAs	Regression analysis	CGE (and SAM)	Micro enterprises/ livelihoods analysis	Local economic mapping (pro-poor value chain analysis)	Master planning	Conventional value chain analysis
Size of tourism-related economy	★★★	★★★	★	★★		★	★	
Competitiveness of tourism sector	★	★	★	★		★	★★★★	★★★
Impact of tourism on macro-economy	★★★	★★	★★★	★★★			★	
Impact of tourism on poor people			★	★/★★★	★★★	★★★	★	
Geographical scale	Regional/ National	National	National/ international	Regional/ National	Local	Destination	National	Tourist product
Policy relevance	★	★	★	★★★★	★★★★	★★★	★★★★	
Extent of application	Widespread	Growing considerably	Widespread	Limited	Limited	Very limited	Everywhere	Very limited
Consideration of:								
• Non-financial issue	No	No	No	No	★★	Some	Few	No
• Direct effects	★★	★★	★★	★★	Some	★★	★	★★
• Secondary effects	No	No	Some	Some	No	Some	Some	No
• Dynamic effects							Few	
Cost	Modest	High	Modest	Reasonable	Modest	Modest	High	Reasonable
Implemented by	Academics	Public bodies/ consultants	Academics	Academics	Researchers/ practitioners	Researchers	Consultants	Consultants/ academics

Blank indicates no relevance; ★ indicates some relevance; ★★ indicates high relevance; ★★★ indicates primary focus.

2   Reflected, for example, in the capability index and human poverty index of the United Nations Development Programme (UNDP). See UNDP, 1996; UNDP, 1997; McKinley, 2006.
3   TSAs have been, by a wide margin, the most important subject of articles to the journal *Tourism Economics* over the past decade. See Wanhill, 2007.

2
The Three Pathways:
Understanding How Tourism
Affects the Poor

While preparing this book, it became clear to us that many researchers have got themselves into a bit of a rut. There are pockets of excellent research going on in almost complete isolation from each other. Tourism master plans rarely cite any academic literature. Many pro-poor tourism practitioners are completely unaware of the recent advances made in equilibrium modelling. This fragmentation is dangerous because, as illustrated in Chapter 1, approaches are not only diverse but also partial. So, by failing to look beyond the confines of any one approach, tourism researchers are not only failing to keep abreast of how others are looking at the same issue from a slightly different angle – but risk losing sight of the 'big picture' itself. Because tourism has a multitude of different effects on the economy – and poor people within it – it is important to keep this broad canvas in mind when zooming into one particular approach to a specific part of this picture. A conceptual model of the different ways tourism can affect poor people has been developed partly to represent this 'big picture'. It also aims to simplify this complex reality into a series of manageable categories in the form of 'pathways'.

There are three key pathways by which the benefits (or costs) of tourism activity can be transmitted to the poor:

1   Direct effects of tourism on the poor: these include both labour income and other forms of earnings from the tourism sector (i.e. jobs in hotels and restaurants, taxi rides). It also includes direct effects from tourism on the poor even if they are non-financial livelihood changes (improved infrastructure or reduced access to the beach for local residents).
2   Secondary effects of tourism on the poor: this includes indirect earnings (and non-financial livelihood impacts) from non-tourism sectors that arise from tourist activity (crafters, construction workers, farmers, etc.). Also included are induced effects from tourism workers who re-spend their earnings in the local economy.

3 Dynamic effects: this broad category covers long-term changes in the economy and patterns of growth whether experienced in the macro economy, or limited to the local economy at the destination. Some environmental impacts, such as the erosion of natural assets from tourist developments, can be conceived as dynamic effects.

Most studies examining the impact of tourism on poverty examine the impact of one of these pathways and a few look at two pathways. This review has not found a rich vein of literature that encompasses them all.

The three pathways are not water-tight categories and the precise location of boundaries can always be contested. The distinction between pathways 1 and 2 can rest either on who spends the money (the tourists or a tourist business), or on the sector into which the business falls (tourism or non-tourism), as elaborated in Chapter 5. Impacts on the poor via government tax revenue also straddle boundaries, leading to direct effects (pathway 1) when park fees collected are shared directly with local communities and dynamic flows (pathway 3) when the revenue raised from taxes paid in the previous period influences spending in the current year.

However, the point of defining the three pathways is not to get bogged down in border disputes. The most urgent goal is to help researchers, policy makers, civil society organizations and others realize that they have been missing at least one vital piece in the jigsaw. Before presenting the evidence from the literature, each pathway is explained in more detail.

Pathway 1: Direct effects of tourism on the poor

Direct earnings occur when poor people receive a flow of financial benefits from engagement in the tourism sector. These can be divided into labour income and non-labour income. Labour income is earnings of individuals in one of two forms: wages from formal sector employment, or earnings from informal sector and micro enterprise activity. Non-labour income includes community income, such as from leases, equity or royalties, and benefits gained through philanthropy directly from the tourism sector.[1]

The earnings are 'direct' if they come from participation in the tourism sector, whether or not the poor person engages face to face with the tourist. Direct earnings clearly involve, for instance, workers in hotels and restaurants, taxi drivers, operators of bed and breakfasts, campsites, canteens or tea shops. Using broader definitions of the tourism sector, a host of providers of recreational, leisure and shopping services, such as local guides and craft sellers may also be included.

Virtually all of the micro-level analyses of tourism and all those focusing on impacts on the poor measure these direct earnings, either at a household or destination level. Analyses focusing on the size or competitiveness of the tourism sector do not specifically assess earnings of the poor, while those assessing economic impact do so only occasionally.

There is a range of direct livelihood impacts on poor people from tourism which occur without a financial transaction. For instance, tourist beach developments may obstruct local fishermen from accessing the main source of their livelihood, the sea, as in Sharm El Sheikh (Goodwin, 2006a). The designation of protected areas can also, simultaneously, deny poor communities access to sources of livelihood and result in animals escaping from the protected area coming into conflict with surrounding villagers (Hatfield, 2005; O'Connell, 1995). The very fact that a household is earning money from tourism may change its exposure to risk (either reducing it via diversification, or increasing it if it becomes reliant on tourism in destinations experiencing volatile demand). Through participation in tourism, poor people may learn skills that they can apply in other ways to boost their livelihoods.

These livelihood impacts are generally well covered in the literature on community-based tourism, conservation and tourism, and in sustainable livelihoods analyses of tourism at the enterprise or community level. They are generally totally absent from other analyses, and thus from most evidence used to inform public policy decision making.

Pathway 2: Secondary effects of tourism on the poor

Secondary effects comprise indirect and induced effects. Indirect effects occur where a change in tourism expenditure impacts on the non-tourism economy. Intuitively, indirect benefits are often conceptualized as supply chain linkages, such as food sales to restaurants. In practice, however, measurement is often based on the fact that the supplier comes from the non-tourism economy, rather than the nature of the transaction. Thus if the 'retail sector' is defined as being outside tourism, then all retail outlets and street vendors who sell to tourists should be regarded as 'indirect' earners.

Another form of secondary earnings is termed 'induced' effects. This arises when workers in the tourism sector spend their earnings locally, thus generating further income for poor households.

Livelihood effects that are indirectly caused by the impact of tourist activity on the non-tourist economy can be significant. For instance, the malnutrition in coastal communities in the Philippines resulted from the collapse of fish stocks due largely to their overexploitation (Mitchell and Shepherd, 2006). In specific instances, tourist demand has accelerated the rate of overexploitation of natural assets, like fish stocks.

Tracing the effects of a change in one part of the economy on other economic variables is not easy. A major contribution of economists to tourism research has been the more systematic treatment of linkages between the tourist and non-tourist economy, through I–O models, VCA, SAMs and CGE models. Traditionally, both the tourism master planning exercises and the micro-level analyses have paid insufficient attention both to the inter-sector linkages and to the role of the poor in supply chains.

This myopia is problematic. Indirect linkages cannot only substantially magnify our understanding of the economic significance of tourism, but can also be a particularly effective way of transmitting the benefits of tourism to very large numbers of very poor people.

Pathway 3: Dynamic effects in the economy and growth trajectories

A delicious irony is that parts of the tourism research literature have been so preoccupied with demonstrating the economic significance of tourism that little thought has been given to the impact of tourism on the structure of the wider economy. Tourist development can have important impacts on the markets and public goods, which may determine the wider opportunities faced by the poor. Poignant that, whilst asserting the dynamism of the tourism sector, almost all tourist research in developing countries has been essentially static – assessing the one-off changes resulting from changes in tourism expenditure. A critical piece of the jig-saw puzzle has been left out.

These dynamic effects are less tangible than direct (pathway 1) and secondary (pathway 2) effects, but are important because they may reinforce – or undermine – the positive impacts of tourism on poor people well beyond the confines of the tourist destination. For example, many poor people in Africa depend for their livelihood on the production of traditional crops for the export market. Researchers have modelled the impact of a boom in tourist expenditure on the rural poor in Tanzania (Kweka 2004; Blake et al, 2008). Under certain conditions, pro-poor gains generated within tourism may be more than offset by the deleterious impact on agricultural competitiveness resulting from a tourist-driven appreciation of the real exchange rate. In other words, the very success of attracting international tourist receipts may undermine the livelihoods of the poor majority who participate in the non-tourism economy.

This has given rise to an embryonic literature on tourism booms and 'Dutch disease'. This framework has traditionally been applied to booms in commodity exports, such as a supply shock like the discovery of oil, where a vulnerable economy may suddenly be swamped with large volumes of foreign exchange. Although this may sound pretty appealing, evidence suggests that – as a result of a range of economic and political factors – many economies are damaged by this phenomenon. Researchers have shown that, in addition to the environmental, social and cultural costs often recognized in the research literature, an inbound tourism boom can, under specific conditions, generate economic costs. At times these costs could be so significant that they result in the immiserization of the host community (Sahli and Nowak, 2005).

On the other hand, tourism may catalyse improvement in human resources by also enhancing women's integration in the economic networks, technical change, economic diversification and infrastructure that provide positive spill-over effects for the poor in other sectors (Lejárraga and Walkenhorst, 2006). While skills and infrastructure development feature prominently in the sustainable livelihoods literature, they are neglected elsewhere. Tourism can also be a major contributor to the tax take of government, which can potentially catalyse fiscal changes that benefit the poor. The relationship between tourism development and economic growth is a subject of many econometric and regression analyses. If tourist expansion stimulates a broader economic dynamism, this could be significant for the poor beyond the tourism sector.

Some of these dynamic effects, such as changes in exchange rates, will affect the whole economy and thus have implications for many poor households who may never see a tourist. Others will be felt particularly within the economy of the destination. Where impacts are concentrated, they can be viewed in terms of how tourism affects local economic development. There is a small, but growing, literature examining the local economic development potential or impacts of tourism. This identifies many similar types of impacts, but from the perspective of the locality rather than the macro-economy.

Many of the dynamic effects, highlighted here in relation to tourist development, could also result from buoyant growth in other sectors of the economy. For instance, rarely is the textile sector criticized for having a positive impact on export earnings and, hence, upward pressure on the real exchange rate and prices. More often the resulting favourable terms of trade are correctly recognized as generating a welfare gain for consumers.

Why foreign exchange earned from textiles is a 'good thing' and foreign exchange earned through tourism is not, presumably reflects an evaluation of the balance of costs and benefits that these two different economic activities impose on the economy. In Chapter 6, dynamic costs and benefits are discussed in greater detail to facilitate an understanding of some of the implicit value judgements that creep into these analyses of the merits of the development of tourism compared with other sectors of the economy.

Figure 2.1 provides a conceptual model of the three pathways by which tourism can affect poor people.

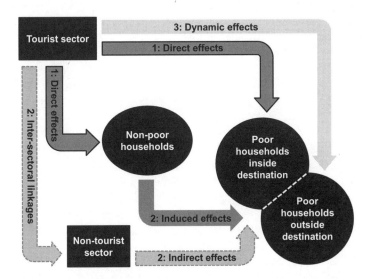

Figure 2.1 *Three pathways of benefits to the poor from tourism*

This conceptual model will be used as a framework to structure the evidence from research in the tourism literature:

- Chapter 3 examines the scale of total benefit flows from tourism to the poor.
- Chapter 4 examines evidence of the direct effects of tourism (pathway 1).
- Chapter 5 assesses research findings on the indirect and induced effects of tourism on the poor (pathway 2).
- Chapter 6 focuses on the dynamic effects of tourism on macro- and local economies (pathway 3).

Empirically, whilst few studies look at the big picture of aggregate benefit flows, many of them offer insights into one of the three main pathways for pro-poor tourism benefit flows. The aim is to understand the significance and relevance of each part of this overall picture.

Notes

1 Since 1999, the pro-poor tourism literature has distinguished three types of earnings: formal sector wages, micro enterprise earnings and collective (community) income, for the very practical reasons that they are generated from different activities, reach different numbers and types of people, and are influenced by different interventions by households, practitioners, companies or government (Ashley et al, 2001) Economists, on the other hand, distinguish factor incomes to labour from factor incomes to capital. The distinctions used here combine both the labour versus non-labour distinction, and the more subtle pro-poor tourism differences based on how it is earned and by whom.

3
The Scale of Flows to the Poor

It is surprising that, despite a huge literature related to tourism and poverty reduction, very few studies can answer the seemingly simple question which lies at the heart of the pro-poor tourism debate: 'What share of the financial benefits of tourism is enjoyed by poor people?' This section marshals the limited evidence available to assess the aggregate flow of income from tourism to poor people, before examining each of the pathways in turn.

There is limited, but emerging, empirical evidence that a substantial amount of the financial flows generated by tourism can accrue to poor households (Mullins and Mulder, 2003; Turpie et al, 2004; Ashley, 2006b; Mitchell and Faal, 2007; Mitchell and Le Chi, 2007; Blake et al, 2008; Mitchell, 2008; Mitchell et al, 2009; Mitchell and Coles, 2009; Coles and Mitchell, 2009; ODI and UNDP, 2009).[1] Interestingly, these studies have analysed different tourist niches (nature based, cultural and beach); contrasting geographical areas (from Southeast Asia to southern Africa) and different types of tourism (from independent to package and from wholly international to a blend of domestic and overseas tourists) (see Figure 3.1).

A detailed study of the tourism value chain in Luang Prabang, a World Heritage Site in northern Laos, concluded that benefits earned by the poor are equivalent to approximately 27 per cent of total tourism expenditure within the destination. The poor are defined here as the informal sector and unskilled and semi-skilled workers – a broad definition in Lao terms, though still more restrictive than the internationally accepted definition of extreme income poverty equivalent to US$1 per head per day (Ashley, 2006a) This result seems to lie at the higher end of the spectrum, as the definition of the poor is broad (looking beyond the poorest of the poor to people who clearly have productive livelihoods, albeit on low incomes), while the tourism expenditure is only the net amount that reaches the destination (measured net of booking fees).

A World Bank study using a SAM in the nature tourism areas of northern KwaZulu-Natal Province in South Africa found that benefits accruing to 'fairly poor' people (unskilled and semi-skilled workers together with small enterprises and communities) amounted to 37 per cent of tourist expenditure in the wildlife areas. Applying a more restrictive definition of the 'poor' – excluding small enterprises and semi-skilled workers – reduced the share of the tourism benefits enjoyed by the poor to 20 per cent (Mullins and Mulder, 2003).

Around the protected areas (meaning game parks) of Namibia another SAM analysis revealed that benefits to the poor amount to around 17 per cent of total tourism turnover at the parks (Turpie et al, 2004). That this estimate is conservative is revealed by the Namibian government's examination of the distributional consequences of increased investment in Namibia's protected areas. It is projected that 23 per cent of economic income generated as a result of these proposed investments in the parks, will benefit poor households in the vicinity of the protected area (Republic of Namibia, 2006).

A study of the 'winter sun' mainstream holiday package value chain in The Gambia, West Africa, estimated that flows to poor people in the form of wages or enterprise earnings are 14 per cent of tourism expenditure in the destination (Mitchell and Faal, 2007). As in Laos, the main channels for pro-poor impact are indirect linkages and specifically, the craft, excursion and food supply chains.

Bwindi and Virunga forests – home to mountain gorillas – in East and Central Africa provide a context with unfavourable conditions for the poor: with park fees of hundreds of dollars a day, government automatically captures around a third of tourist spending, while local people have little beyond their labour to sell. An assessment by Hatfield and Malleret-King (2007) focused on the full range of benefits from conservation, in which international benefits far outweigh local ones. But local income as a share of tourist's in-country spending was not so negligible. Direct and indirect flows to community members, amounted to roughly 10 per cent or more of in-country tourist spending. The figure is neither exact nor strictly comparable (high due to assumed multipliers, low due to the narrow community of focus and variable depending on whether local or national expenditure is used) but indicates likely income shares at one end of the range.

A more urban example of more significant tourist flows that have very limited destination impact is Siem Reap, the city around the Anghor Wat temples in Cambodia. Some 1.5 million visitors generate about US$300 million annual tourist expenditure of which only about 7 per cent flows to poor people in the local area. This low share reflects poorly developed linkages between the tourism value chain and local communities, exacerbated by a severely disenabling environment established by government (ODI and UNDP, 2009). More recent work on conference tourism in Accra, Ghana indicates that only about 10 per cent of tourism expenditure accrues to the local community. Craft spending is low, much of the food consumed by tourists is imported and few hotel workers are from poor backgrounds. In Accra, sex workers are the main resource-poor beneficiaries of conference tourism.

It is likely that the share of tourism revenue reaching the poor at the destination rarely falls below the 6 per cent level. Even in destinations with very low wage rates, non-management staff wages constitute 6 per cent of total tourist spending across a broad range of destinations. Once other earnings of

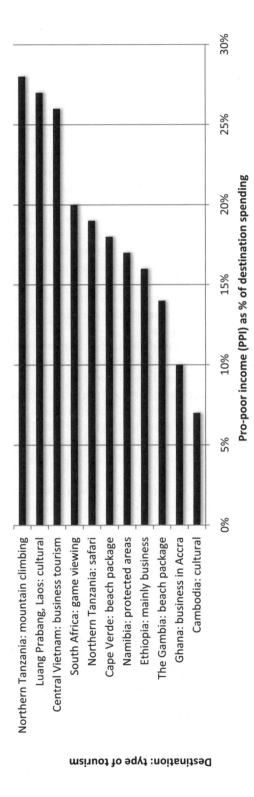

Destination: type of tourism

Northern Tanzania: mountain climbing
Luang Prabang, Laos: cultural
Central Vietnam: business tourism
South Africa: game viewing
Northern Tanzania: safari
Cape Verde: beach package
Namibia: protected areas
Ethiopia: mainly business
The Gambia: beach package
Ghana: business in Accra
Cambodia: cultural

Pro-poor income (PPI) as % of destination spending

0%   5%   10%   15%   20%   25%   30%

Source: Coles and Mitchell, 2009

Figure 3.1 *Total income earned by the poor as a percentage of total tourism expenditure in the destination*

the poor from employment or enterprise, plus indirect and induced effects, are included, it would be difficult to conceive of benefits not exceeding this level.

An innovative CGE analysis of tourism and poverty in Brazil also examines the distributional effects of tourism. The lowest income and low-income households together receive almost half the household earnings from tourism in Brazil (Blake et al, 2008).

Although this is clearly a narrow empirical foundation from which to generalize about the distributional impacts of a sector of the economy, some initial indications that emerge from comparing these results include the following.

First, the extent to which tourist activity benefits the poor varies considerably from place to place. At the upper end of the scale, benefits equivalent to one-quarter of the total tourist expenditure taking place in a destination reach the poor either directly or indirectly (wages for workers, earnings for micro and small enterprises (MSEs) in the tourism sector or the supply chain, and rentals and leases for communities). Different factors seem to be responsible for this:

- In southern Africa, unskilled wage rates are unusually high, and account for the bulk of pro-poor benefit flows.
- In parts of Southeast Asia wage rates are much lower, but there is a thriving small enterprise sector and craft industry and a reasonable share of the food supplied to the tourism sector is grown locally.
- Specific features of particular value chains matter. For instance, the labour-intensity of guides, porters and cooks accompanying tourists climbing Mount Kilimanjaro is the main reason that the climbing package in Northern Tanzania is so much more pro-poor than the safari package in the same region.

Elsewhere, the scale of pro-poor benefit flow is lower. In the example from Central Africa only one-tenth of the cash benefits of tourism accrue to the poor. This is observed in the context of extreme rural poverty, which constrains local supply capacity, and high prices that reflect the scarcity value of gorillas. The capture of tourism benefits by local communities is poor in Cambodia and Accra because of an enabling environment that encourages elite capture and militates against the poor engaging successfully with the tourism value chain.

Second, the importance of being precise about the definition of poverty is highlighted by the findings from the study in northern **KwaZulu-Natal** (Mullins and Mulder, 2003). Whether or not semi-skilled workers and small business are included or excluded significantly affects the share of tourism captured by the 'poor'. In the **KwaZulu-Natal** study, the share of tourism expenditure received by the poor jumps from 20 per cent to 37 per cent depending on how poverty is defined.

Third, this analysis questions the bold assertion made in parts of the critical tourism studies literature that: 'tourism does not benefit the poor'. In all the destinations where researchers have looked – even in highly disadvantageous circumstances – there are significant benefit flows from tourism to poor people.

What the analysis suggests, therefore, is that some benefits do flow from tourism to the poor and that the share received by the poor varies considerably.

There is virtually no information on what difference these cash benefits from tourism make to poverty levels around tourist destinations, or of how they compare with non-financial and dynamic effects. Indictors of the significance of earnings to poverty levels are generally limited to micro-level analyses.

Examples of the impact that tourism benefits have on poverty levels are patchy and include:

- At village level, total household income can increase dramatically as a result of tourism activity. Surveys by the Mekong Tourism Development Programme in villages around a successful tourist excursion in Luang Prabang in Laos report that average household income increased almost fourfold between 2004 and 2005 (LNTA, 2005).
- One of the very few analyses that assess impacts at the local level using a control group, is an assessment in Namibia of how the incomes of households in conservancies (community institutions managing tourism and wildlife) compared with those outside conservancies. This involved a multivariate analysis of 1192 households in seven conservancy areas in two regions of Namibia, (Bandyopadhyay et al, 2004). The analysis found that on average, households living in the Kunene and Caprivi conservancies experienced 29 per cent and 58 per cent higher per capita income respectively than households living outside the established conservancies. Moreover, poor and female-headed households were found to benefit equally or even disproportionately from these conservancy-related gains.

Simply calculating the aggregate share of tourist expenditure that reaches the poor tells us little about how the benefits are transmitted and how they can be increased. It also underestimates (or misses out on) a range of non-financial effects, ranging from immediate changes in livelihood assets, to long-term changes in the growth trajectory of the macro-economy. In Chapters 4 to 6 the evidence available for each pathway is considered in further detail.

Note

1 As noted below, these studies differ somewhat in what is included in 'benefits to the poor', and probably also in measurement of 'expenditure within the destination', so the percentages presented for benefits to the poor relative to total spend are not entirely comparable.

4
Pathway 1: Direct Effects of Tourism on the Poor

The aim of this chapter is to summarize the findings from the literature regarding the direct effects of tourism on the poor. These benefit flows accrue mainly to poor households within, or near to, a tourism destination.

The direct effects of tourism on the poor are labour income, non-labour income and livelihood effects. The former is divided into wages from formal sector employment and income from informal, micro and small enterprises. Non-labour income is divided into different types of community collective income. Evidence of non-financial livelihood effects is also considered.

Labour income: Wages from formal sector employment

This section outlines evidence on the importance of tourism employment to the poor, and considers evidence on labour intensity, wage rates and working conditions, and factors that influence the scale of employment benefits.

Box 4.1 *Meaning of formal sector employment*

This section focuses on the earnings of the poor from formal sector employment, which is contrasted with earnings from self-employment, individual entrepreneurship or micro-enterprise. This is different from usage of the term 'employment' in a macro-economic context, which would normally include self-employment. Here self-employment is considered as a separate form of labour income, put in the following section because of the different people, impacts and policy issues involved.

Formal sector employment is a critical pathway by which resources flow from tourists through suppliers (hotels, restaurants, transport companies, etc.) to the poor. Employment in the hospitality sector is often regarded as the main contribution of the benefits of tourism to less skilled households.

For example, in tourism master plans and policy documents, whilst data on other types of linkage between tourism and the poor are often sporadic, there are invariably headline data about the number of jobs created by tourism (CHL Consulting, 2002; Crompton and Christie, 2003). The only data that are commonly available in countries are these headline data, and the quoted or imputed resulting figures for arrivals per job, and/or jobs per hotel room. The former is generally in the range of 20 to 50 tourists per job, while jobs per room range from around 0.3 to 2, depending on type of accommodation – with an average of around one full time equivalent job generated per hotel room. It is often assumed that many of these opportunities are for disadvantaged households.

The evidence suggests formal sector tourism employment ranges from 12 to 76 per cent of the total income from tourism to the poor – a tremendous variation.

In countries with generous minimum wage legislation (South Africa) or a tightening labour market (Cape Verde) or highly skilled staff (safari driver guides in Tanzania), formal sector wages often account for the bulk of direct benefit flows to the poor (Relly 2004b; Massyn and Koch, 2004a). In this context, the difference waged employment makes to the well-being of the poor is dramatic and will often lift a family out of poverty on a sustainable basis (Poultney and Spenceley, 2001). In other countries, formal sector wages constitute a high share of pro-poor benefits not because hotel workers are well paid or skilled but rather because the volume of pro-poor benefits is so limited, as in Cambodia.

However, in other countries formal sector employment accounts for a much more modest share of pro-poor income. In a typical low-income country environment, formal sector wages may vary from $35 to $100 a month (see Table 4.1). Even where tips are included, formal sector wages will be a much less significant channel for the transmission of pro-poor benefits where wages are so low – as is the case in The Gambia, Laos and Ethiopia.

The second caveat is that this analysis is highly contingent on how one defines poverty. In our early studies, we sought to justify formal sector wages as a pro-poor benefit by demonstrating that they were below the international income poverty line. The implications of this approach are perverse, that incomes to poor communities cease to be a pro-poor benefit if employers reward employees at above-poverty wage levels. It is for this reason that we are now using dynamic definitions of poverty that look at the background of workers, rather than their current earnings, to determine whether tourism has contributed to the reduction of poverty.

It can be argued that those who manage to secure jobs in the tourism sector tend to be those with language skills, connections and some education. The evidence suggests that many non-management tourist workers are poor in

Table 4.1 *Wage employment and the poor*

		Source
What share of total pro-poor income is generated by formal sector employment?	Namibia: 76%	Turpie et al, 2004
	Tanzania: 75%	Mitchell et al, 2009
	South Africa (Madikwe): 68%	Relly, 2004a
	Cape Verde: 52%	Mitchell, 2008
	Cambodia: 48%	ODI and UNDP, 2009
	Brazil: 31–49%	Blake et al, 2008
	The Gambia: 17%	Mitchell and Faal, 2008
	Laos (Luang Prabang): 12%	Ashley, 2006a
What percentage of tourism jobs go to the poor?	*Unskilled*	
	Malawi: 56%	Christie, 2006
	Maldives: 45%	World Bank, 2006a
	'Local' residents	
	Ethiopia (Lalibela): 100%	Mitchell and Coles, 2009
	Ethiopia (Addis Ababa): 88%	Mitchell and Coles, 2009
	Ghana (Accra) 20%	Coles and Mitchell, 2009
What percentage of the tourism wage bill is captured by the poor?	*Unskilled*	
	Namibia: 54%	Turpie et al, 2004
	South Africa (KwaZulu-Natal): 46%	Aylward and Lutz, 2003
	Malawi: 18%	Christie and Crompton, 2001
	Brazil: 17%	Blake et al, 2008
	Unskilled and semi-skilled	
	The Gambia 85%	Mitchell and Faal, 2008
	South Africa (KwaZulu-Natal): 70%	Aylward and Lutz, 2003
	Brazil 27%	Blake et al, 2008
	'Local' residents	
	South Africa (KwaZulu-Natal): 73%	Aylward and Lutz, 2003
	South Africa (Madikwe): 55%	Relly, 2004a

Box 4.2 *The impact of tourism employment on village income*

In the 1990s, villagers around the newly established Madikwe Game Reserve (in the North-West Province of South Africa) earned roughly US$2.6 million from all activities, excluding commercial farming. By 2003, when bed capacity in the new reserve had reached 386, it was estimated that residents were earning $1.3–1.6 million per annum from tourism. Thus their total village income had increased by between 50 and 62 per cent from tourism – even while the reserve and the tourism-linked economy were still developing. Local tourist wages are about three times the average household income in the area and 50 per cent of the wage bill is received by women (based on Relly 2004a supplemented with data from Massyn and Koch, 2004b, 2004a).

international terms, although they are often not the poorest in their countries. For example, in hotels in Malawi, 43 per cent of staff have no more than primary education and 42 per cent of staff are 'unskilled' (Chikosi et al, 2006). In some remote locations, necessity and the need for 'social license to operate' can result in 80 to 90 per cent of staff being recruited from rural and relatively unskilled communities (Massyn and Koch, 2004a; Relly 2004a).

The percentage of women in employment varies considerably (see Box 4.3). It is often noted to be around 50 per cent, and the fact that women are earning income directly makes a further contribution to the well-being of households.

Those in regular employment are self-evidently living at the tourism destination for at least part of the year. However, this does not necessarily mean that formal sector employment only benefits poor households within a destination, as migration to work in tourism is common, though rarely measured.

One comprehensive assessment in Cambodia indicates the scale of remittances from workers in the tourist sector (see Table 4.2). Notwithstanding the low and gender-biased rates of pay prevailing in the Cambodian hotel sector, the great majority of both men and women remit wages. These amount to a transfer of $1.2 million per month from the main tourist destinations in Siem Reap and Phnom Penh to some of the poorest rural areas in Southeast Asia.

Table 4.2 *Tourism, gender and remittances in Cambodia*

Gender	Sending remittances	No. of respondents	Salary (US$)	Remittance (US$)	Number of staff	Total remittances
	Yes	283 (79%)	77	40 (52%)	25,108	$793,413
Male	No	75 (21%)				
	Total	358				
	Yes	341 (77%)	53	33 (62%)	16,336	$431,270
Female	No	101 (23%)				
	Total	442				

Source: ODI and UNDP, 2009

Tourism wages, working conditions and labour markets

The levels of wages earned by unskilled and semi-skilled workers in the tourism sector vary enormously by region. There is a common view in the literature that tourism creates a highly exploited and vulnerable workforce (Weru, 2007; Slob and Wilde-Ramsing, 2006; Hampton and Christensen, 2005; Mtui, 2007; Wagner, 1997).

In a tourism VCA in northeast Brazil, Slob and Wilde-Ramsing (2006) point to the feminization of the workforce; the extent of temporary contracts and irregular hours; the lack of career progression and the low level of unionization of the tourism sector – below 10 per cent – in hotels owned by multinational corporations. It is suggested that this exacerbates unethical

---

Box 4.3 *Data on employment of women in tourism*

One of the few types of tourism impact data that are disaggregated by gender are employment data. As a percentage of lodge/hotel employees in southern African destinations, women account for 65 per cent in Rocktail Bay Lodge in KwaZulu-Natal (Poultney and Spenceley, 2001), 55 per cent in Dullstroom hotels on the Mpumalanga Escarpment (Rogerson, 2002) and 59 per cent in Madikwe Game Reserve lodges (Relly 2004a). In Zambia, women account for 30 per cent of total staff in hotels in Livingstone, with the ratio of male to female workers almost equal (48 per cent) in guest houses (DCDM Consulting, 2006).

Moving on to national-level data, Page (1999) estimates that women account for about half of tourism employees in South Africa largely concentrated in the hotel and restaurant sectors, with a very small percentage employed in transportation.

In the Philippines in 1998, more women than men were employed in the tourism industry on aggregate. However, retail trade is dominated by female employees (82 per cent) as opposed to entertainment and cultural services which attract more men extensively (Virola et al, 2001).

Employment patterns are, however, culturally defined. In countries in North and West Africa, the tourism workforce is sometimes almost exclusively men.

The United Nations compiled data on women's employment for submission to the Commission on Sustainable Development in 1999. The general picture suggests that the tourism industry is a particularly important sector for generating employment opportunities for women with 46 per cent of the tourism workforce comprising women. This percentage, however, varies greatly between different countries ranging from 2 per cent to over 80 per cent (UNED-UK, 1999).

---

labour and unsustainable management in the local tourism industry. In Brazil, Wagner (1997) finds that the majority of tourism-related jobs are in the service and commercial sectors where wages are not much better than those earned by subsistence and low-income households, and so will do nothing to break the cycle of poverty. Hampton and Christensen (2005) state that tourism is typically poorly paid relative to other industries. It is common for staff to be laid off in the low season, or to be underemployed. The conditions of work are poor, with tourism involving hard, physical labour and long, anti-social hours.

By contrast, Christie and Crompton (2001) note that the contribution of tourism to the creation of decent jobs is often better than assumed. Christie and Crompton (2003) suggest that tourism not only creates jobs but it establishes 'good jobs' characterized by healthier, safer and more pleasant working conditions than other sectors of the economy.

Service jobs in hotels are relatively well paid, particularly when supplemented by tips. In an analysis of the small hotel sector in the Arusha region in Tanzania, Sharma (2003) found that hotel workers are paid 15–20 per cent more than comparative professions. Lengefeld and Beyer (2006) calculated that hotel wages in Nicaragua appeared lower than those in a nearby sugar factory ($119 per month compared with $134). However, the majority of hotel staff are on permanent contracts and enjoy a benefits package that includes a 13th cheque, paid leave and other benefits. In Kenya, Summary (1987) found that wages paid in the tourism industry were below the average for the modern economy as a whole.

Choy (1995) analyses the quality of tourism employment using Hawaii as a case example. The analysis shows that service industries in Hawaii are the largest source (31 per cent) of managerial positions and second largest source (40 per cent) of professional and technical positions. The perception that the tourist industry offers mostly low-skill occupations is challenged by the finding that a significant proportion (25–30 per cent) of these service positions are supervisory or skilled occupations.

Table 4.3 provides some indicative annual wage levels for non-managerial hotel jobs and illustrates the considerable variability between countries. In the atypical southern African labour market, wages are sufficient to keep a family above the international '$1 a day' extreme income poverty line. Elsewhere non-managerial wages may meet locally defined poverty thresholds, but generally cannot lift an average family over the international poverty line.

However, the key comparison when assessing tourism wages is how these compare with the opportunity cost of labour – or what other kind of jobs would be available should workers leave the tourist sector. Only in a small number of developing countries does the opportunity cost of labour approach the level of tourism wages.

In some cases these do not include tips or non-cash benefits, which in some destinations provide a significant addition. For example, in The Gambia, they can add 50 per cent to the monthly salary for employees (Mitchell and Faal, 2008) and 22 per cent in the Caribbean (Lengefeld and Beyer, 2006).

Table 4.3 *Selected tourism wages*

Country (destination)	Average US$ per year for non-managerial workers	Source
Cape Verde	4900	Mitchell, 2008
Zambia (Livingstone accommodation)	1650	DCDM Consulting, 2006
Zambia (Livingstone activity companies)	3050	DCDM Consulting, 2006
Tunisia (large beach and business hotels)	2750	UNCTAD, 2007
Caribbean (all-inclusive resorts)	1050–1670	Lengefeld and Beyer, 2006
Ghana (Accra)	1452	Coles and Mitchell, 2009
Egypt (Sharm El Sheikh)	1347	Goodwin, 2006a
The Gambia	1128	Mitchell and Faal, 2008
Ethiopia	920	Mitchell and Coles, 2009
Laos (Luang Prabang guest houses)	440	Ashley, 2006a
Laos (Luang Prabang hotels)	840	
Namibia (community-based campsites)	516	Halstead, 2003

Wages earned by the poor also emerge as a substantial proportion of the total tourism payroll, despite the fact that the unskilled and semi-skilled often earn much lower wages than other staff. The ratio of management to non-management wages varies widely. In the hotel sector in central Vietnam, for instance, management remuneration is only about twice the level of semi-skilled non-management staff (Mitchell and Le Chi, 2007). By contrast, in Malawi, managers receive salaries at a large ratio of the level of unskilled wages (Christie and Crompton, 2001).

In summary, there is little consensus about the quality of tourism employment and wages of the poor. Much depends on the specific country, its labour market and tourism seasonality, and on whether the comparison is with desired norms, other sectors, or other countries. There is a reasonably strong empirical case for making two seemingly contradictory assessments on this issue. First, tourist wages are generally attractive in comparison with the alternatives available in many developing countries. Second, looking beyond the aberrant labour markets in southern Africa and the Caribbean, unskilled and semi-skilled tourist wages are very low when judged by the standards prevailing in main tourism source markets.

Labour intensity and shares to unskilled labour

The pro-poor credentials of tourism are often justified on the basis of the high labour intensity of the sector. Many claims stem from an analysis that found that tourism is more labour intensive than other non-agricultural sectors and manufacturing in particular (Bennett et al, 1999). The statistics of a cross-country analysis of the labour intensity in various sectors is summarized in Table 4.4 where the labour rich nature of the tourism industry is confirmed.

If tourism is compared to the average developing country economy, it does not appear particularly labour intensive. National averages are strongly influenced by agriculture. As Table 4.4 also shows, agriculture is significantly more labour intensive than either tourism or other sectors (except in Kenya where the data follow a pattern that contrasts with everywhere else and is counter intuitive). Agriculture is typically between two to five times more labour intensive than tourism.

The labour intensity of tourism in comparison to the whole economy is low in much of Africa because the non-tourist economy is dominated by agriculture. As economies develop towards middle-income status, the labour intensity of tourism, relative to the rest of the economy, increases. The labour intensity of tourism may not have changed, but the average labour intensity for the economy decreases as the non-tourist economy makes the transition to a more productive and less agriculturally dependent model. In Table 4.4 this trend is clear for Asia over the period from 1990 to 2005, as these dynamic economies industrialize. The absence of this trend in Africa, reflecting the failure of the continent to move beyond its primary commodity dependency, is striking.

Table 4.4 Labour intensity in tourism compared with other sectors

Country/Region	1990–1995			1996–2000			2001–2005		
	Tourism industry	Non-agriculture	Agriculture	Tourism industry	Non-agriculture	Agriculture	Tourism industry	Non-agriculture	Agriculture
Botswana	1.38	0.88	3.57	1.38	0.83	6.35	1.38	0.9	4.47
Ethiopia	0.76	0.16	1.69	0.76	0.42	1.65	0.76		
The Gambia	0.8			0.8			0.8		
Kenya	0.8	1.15	0.64	0.8	1.19	0.58	0.8		
South Africa	1.23	0.78	2.06	1.03	0.9	3.75	1.01	0.93	2.82
Egypt	0.85	0.8		0.85	0.85	1.75	0.85	0.86	1.7
Brazil	1.13	0.8	3.25	1	0.83	3.03	0.96	0.87	2.37
Thailand	0.92	0.47	5.45	0.84	0.56	5.16	0.79	0.6	4.77
Vietnam	0.77	0.41	2.3	0.77	0.46	2.56	0.77	0.49	2.7
New Zealand	1.15	0.97	1.36	1.12	0.98	1.2	1.07	1	0.96
Latin America & Caribbean	1.09	0.89	2.21	1.03	0.89	2.39	1	0.89	2.34
North Africa & Middle East	1.11			0.98			1.05		
Southeast Asia	0.76	0.6	2.51	0.91	0.63	2.81	1.09	0.64	3.28
Sub-Saharan Africa	0.84			0.81			0.76		
Whole Economy	1	1	1	1	1	1	1	1	1

Source: Compiled from World Bank, 2006b and WTTC (no date)

Note: All figures are averages over the period indicated according to data availability. Figures for non-tourism sectors for the period 2001–2005 refer to the period 2001–2003. Tourism industry data refer to employment in hotels, restaurants and transportation only.

Interpretation: The whole economy contributes the same share to output, or GDP (100 per cent) as to employment (100 per cent), so the ratio of its contributions to output and employment is 1. A labour intensive sector would contribute more to employment than to GDP (above average jobs per unit of output), so the employment:output ratio (EOR) would be above 1. The table shows that the EOR for tourism is noticeably higher than the EOR for non-agricultural sectors in general (the average is distorted by the very high EOR of agriculture).

Other indicators of employment creation

Another way of measuring the labour intensity of tourism is in terms of the income of labour as a percentage of factor income (see Table 4.5), which ranges from around 30 per cent to 50 per cent. The Brazilian figure of 87 per cent of factor income accruing to labour (Blake et al, 2008) is clearly an outlier. It may reflect researchers using contrasting definitions of the categories such as 'labour'. For example, in the Brazil study the self-employed are defined as labour. In the Namibian study some inputs provided by poor households – such as farmers and community businesses – are grouped under capital (Turpie et al, 2004).

Table 4.5 *Tourism as a creator of jobs*

		Source
Income to labour as a percentage of all factor income	Brazil 87%	Blake et al, 2008
	Tanzania 46%	Kweka et al, 2003
	KwaZulu-Natal 42%	Mullins and Mulder, 2003
	Namibia 29%	Turpie et al, 2006
Wages as a % of turnover (accommodation sector)	Vietnam 24% (non-management wages)	Mitchell and Le Chi, 2007
	Malawi 17%	Christie, 2006
	Namibia 13%	Turpie et al, 2006
	Zambia 13%	DCDM Consulting, 2006
	Gambia 7% (non-management wages)	Mitchell and Faal, 2008
	Laos 6% (unskilled and semi-skilled)	Ashley, 2006a

From the perspective of the poor, it is not just the labour intensity that matters, but the share of these jobs that are unskilled or semi-skilled and thus accessible to the poor. Limited and anecdotal evidence suggests that tourism is a relatively rich source of these jobs in most places. Reviewing data for Mauritius, South Africa and Zimbabwe, Page (1999) concluded that tourism makes intensive use of unskilled labour. In KwaZulu-Natal, a much greater share of labour income is earned by the unskilled rather than the skilled compared to the rest of the economy (Mullins and Mulder, 2003).

Factors affecting labour income from employment

The nature of tourism affects employment impacts. These data are generally not synthesized or quantified:

- The type of hotel influences the staff:room ratio (Christie and Crompton, 2003; UNCTAD, 2007; Lengefeld and Beyer, 2006; Ashley, 2006a).
- The number of bars and restaurants maintained in the hotel influences the average number of staff per room (Goodwin, 2006a).
- The use of family labour reduces the number of employees. In Luang Prabang most guest houses are managed by family members (Ashley, 2006a). This

brings the reported staff per room ratio in budget guest houses down to just 0.3 per room, compared with 1.3 in the hotels.
- Foreign-owned hotels generally pay slightly higher wages than domestic ones. Limited fieldwork in Rwanda (Verdugo, 2007) and Tunisia (UNCTAD, 2007) suggested this is the case.
- Where 'world pricing' applies to the tourism products while local labour markets determine wage rates, a higher share of national income may occur in the form of profits rather than wages (Page, 1999).

Labour market conditions and government intervention

The labour market in other sectors can influence tourism labour conditions and vice versa. Page (1999) attributes the significant extent of male employment in the tourism sector in South Africa and Zimbabwe to the high levels of male unemployment in these economies. In Mauritius the same phenomenon is observed in the tourism workforce, but for a different reason – the intensive employment of women in the clothing industry in the country.

Government interventions can also influence the final outcomes of the labour market in many ways, thus affecting earnings of the poor. On the supply side, the state has an important role to play in providing good quality training to equip local communities with the skills to contribute productively to the tourism economy (Verdugo, 2007; Weru, 2007). For example, the lack of language and hospitality skills in Mozambique is a barrier to entry for locals to participate in the tourism industry (Sarmento, 2007). Tunisia provides an example where government prioritization of training does appear to have ensured that the vast majority of jobs are taken by Tunisians. There is public training, and also a specific training tax levied on the tourism sector, from which hotels can opt out if they spend the money on training themselves (UNCTAD, 2007; Ashley, 2006b).

On the demand side, government can influence both wage levels and re-cruitment of the poor, to a limited extent. At present, many host governments preside over a regulatory environment that has the effect of undermining any move towards decent wages for tourist workers. In The Gambia, for instance, the criminalization of workplace democracy served to shield employers from pressures to increase wages in the tourist sector (Mitchell and Faal, 2007). However, statutory regulations are not always implemented (Weru, 2007) and the tourism sector is often not regulated by defined wage categories (Mtui, 2007).

Government can also create a conducive environment for the recruitment of poor people and the establishment of decent employment conditions by implementing, for example, labour law, legislation to promote equal opport-unities, affirmative action regulations and incentives for training and em-ployment of 'local people'. Anti-discrimination legislation and practice may also influence the demand for labour from a broader pool of candidates.

However, there is a risk here that regulation may incentivize hotels to adapt their practice to find a way around them. This is the case in some Tunisian hotels where employment agreements are terminated before the completion of the minimum working period – set at four years – after which employees are entitled to a permanent position (UNCTAD, 2007).

There are indications that more progressive employers have an important role in supply-side initiatives that can expand access for the poor. For instance, Sandals (an up-market, Jamaican-owned, all-inclusive resort group based in the Caribbean) has had a corporate commitment to spending $100 per staff member each year and allocating part of these resources to training local youth to allow them to enter the workforce (Lengefeld and Stewart, 2004). In South Africa, many partnerships between local communities and tourist companies have included preferential local employment provisions. These have successfully not only brought an unskilled labour market into the workforce but, with intensive training programmes, rapidly brought formerly unskilled staff into the management cadre. In Brazil's northeast on the Coconut Coast, the Berimbau project (an innovative partnership between the Bank of Brazil and the International Trade Centre (ITC)) resulted in a training initiative that increased local sourcing of staff for a 1,800 bed resort from 10 per cent to 40 per cent of the workforce within a few months. The poverty-reducing impact of the additional $2m in wages flowing into the surrounding communities each year has been dramatic (Mitchell and Ashley, 2008).

Advocacy and campaign groups emphasize the role that tourism suppliers as employers and international tour operators have in encouraging decent wages for tourist workers (Kalisch, 2002). Analyses of the economics of accommodation in the tourist sector often indicate that the payroll is a small element of operating costs – on occasion less significant than food and beverages, provision for depreciation, loan repayments and even energy costs. Some analyses also show the high gross operating margins of many hotels (Mitchell and Faal, 2007).

International tour operators are beginning to respond to the changing customer attitudes in their source markets by seeking to enhance their destination impact. For example, the Federation of Tour Operators' (FTO) (the umbrella organization for the largest outbound tour operators in the UK) *Guidebook on Sustainable Suppliers* encourages suppliers to pay a 'living wage' and respect all minimum wage legislation (FTO, 2006). This initiative should be welcomed because it is likely to drive up labour conditions in formal sector jobs in supplier organizations in developing country destinations. However, it may also present pro-poor tourism practitioners with a dilemma. Whilst driving the adoption of international standards in formal sector occupations in the supply chain may well have a progressive impact, raising standards may also have the effect of reducing opportunities for the informal sector to access the tourist market (Kirsten and Rogerson, 2002).

Labour income: From micro, small and informal tourism businesses

---

Box 4.4 *Defining the term 'micro and small enterprise'*

The term micro and small enterprise – MSE – is used here to include those working in the informal sector, the self-employed, the small entrepreneur, and producers selling goods and services into the tourist value chain. In this section we consider MSEs working in the tourism sector, such as operating a tea shop, providing cultural entertainment, transporting tourists, acting as a guide or offering home stays.

Other MSEs who earn money through the supply chain – and work outside the tourist sector – are considered separately in Chapter 5 on indirect earnings. However, the boundary is not always clear and depends on how tightly the 'tourist sector' is defined. Hence, many studies merge the two types of informal sector.

Earnings and beneficiaries

The main pro-poor significance of the informal sector is that this is where thousands of the poor are able to access the tourism economy. Many of them will be using limited tourism income to supplement a range of other incomes or fill gaps. Sometimes the sums they earn may be small from a national point of view, but the number of poor people that can utilize tourism as one of their livelihood strategies is often surprisingly large.

Tourism's ability to generate employment in the informal sector has been cited as one of the key opportunities presented by tourism growth for developing countries (de Kadt, 1979).

In The Gambia more than 3000 people work in the formal tourism sector. Around this, a reasonably rich network of informal sector tourist businesses has developed which has created productive opportunities for over 1000 entrepreneurs, as Table 4.6 illustrates. About half of these informal sector livelihoods are generated from within the tourism sector, working as guides and taxi drivers (the others, working in the craft and retail sector, whilst totally dependent upon sales to tourists, work outside the tourism sector).

Sometimes individuals working in the informal sector receive lower earnings than formal sector workers contracted in the informal sector – like hotel workers. However, the pattern observed in The Gambia is not unusual with informal sector activities appearing to be better remunerated than jobs in the formal sector.

A striking example of the pro-poor benefit flow from informal workers in the tourist sector is seen in the Mount Kilimanjaro climbing value chain in northern Tanzania. Although a few climbing staff are employed by tour operators, the majority of the estimated 400 guides, 10,000 porters and 500 cooks

Table 4.6 *Tourism and related employment in The Gambia, 2006*

Category of worker	Full-time equivalent workers	Average monthly earnings (US$)
Formal tourist sector		
Hotel workers	2700	94
Ground handlers	289	N/A
Public officials	50	164
Subtotal	*3039*	*262,000*
Informal sector		
Licensed guides	75	218
Licensed tourist taxi drivers	453	212
Licensed craft retailers	384	146
Licensed fruit sellers	150	182
Licensed juice sellers	75	182
Subtotal	*1137*	*208,900*
Total	*4176*	*470,900*

Source: Mitchell & Faal (2007)

Note: For definitional purposes, it can be debated whether juice sellers fall under the 'restaurants' sector within tourism or the 'food sector' without. Similarly, craft sellers fall under the 'retail' sector in the SNA, but are included in the 'tourism economy' using broader definitions.

work in the informal sector. Although working conditions on the mountain are hard and wages are low (from $3.50 to $10.60 a day) 62 per cent of total pro-poor benefits accrue to climbing staff (Mitchell et al, 2009).

It is mainly the employment of very large numbers of informal sector climbing staff which results in the Mount Kilimanjaro climbing value chain being estimated at 28 per cent pro-poor (Mitchell et al, 2009, see Figure 4.1). This is the most successful transfer of resources from international tourists to poor people living around a destination of any of the places we have studied in Africa, Southeast Asia or Latin America.

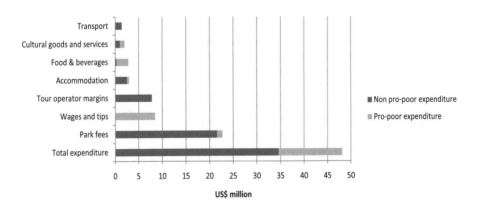

Figure 4.1 *Mount Kilimanjaro, Tanzania, climber expenditure*

Which poor people benefit

Earnings of direct micro and small enterprise income from the tourism sector are generally confined to households within the destination, with the exception of some migrant workers. The exact cut-off between poor and non-poor in this area is difficult to define and it would certainly be unwise to assume that all informal entrepreneurs are resource poor. The informal sector has allowed some workers in the tourism sector to escape poverty for good.

The informal sector is one of the few arenas where some of the poorest households can engage in tourism. Shah and Gupta (1998) point out that vending can provide a relatively low barrier to entering the tourism trade, particularly for the poor and women. Even when informal sector sales are seasonal and unreliable, they can constitute a useful supplement to other livelihood strategies being pursued by poor households – as in Nepal (Saville, 2001) and Namibia (Murphy, 2003).

Factors affecting direct small business income

Tourist discretionary expenditure is a crucial determinant affecting the part-icipation of micro and small enterprises in the tourism economy. This type of expenditure has been described as 'out-of-pocket spending' (Mitchell and Faal, 2007; Ashley, 2006b), 'complementary product spending' (Bah and Goodwin, 2003), or 'expenditure outside the tourist hospitality premises' (Crompton and Christie, 2003). Whatever term is used, the key idea is that the more time and money tourists spend outside resorts, the greater the opportunities for MSEs to respond to this demand.

An analysis of the tourism value chain in Ethiopia (Mann, 2006) found little value being added beyond the profitability of the individual service providers such as tour operators and hotels. Tourists face difficulties in changing money, the quality of crafts is poor and local guiding, facilities and other services are inadequate. As a result, out-of-pocket spending is low and local enterprise is very limited.

Limited tourist discretionary spending in Ethiopia, Mozambique and Uganda is illustrated in Figure 4.2. Although this information is based upon one high-end, specialized tour operator in the UK and cannot be generalized with any reliability (in particular, mainstream operators work on much tighter margins for much greater tourist flows than niche operators), it clearly illustrates the missed opportunities for pro-poor tourism in some of the poorest countries in Africa.

In The Gambia spending on activities and shopping is high relative to other African destinations, and has been increased by a series of destination-level interventions that assist informal sector operators (see, for example, Bah and Goodwin, 2003; Mitchell and Faal, 2007). Despite its modest share of total tourist expenditure, the informal sector constitutes an important transfer of resources from relatively affluent tourists to local people in the destination.

Whilst there is some other literature on the importance of out-of-pocket spending for the poor, there is overall a crippling lack of reliable and

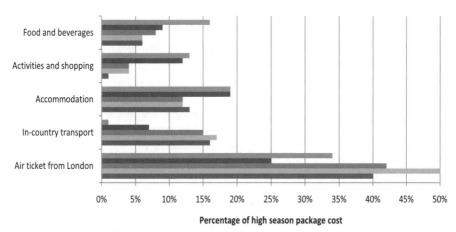

Source: Mann, 2007; Mitchell and Faal, 2008

Note: Figures are based on limited data and included for illustrative purposes only; a more recent analysis of the Ethiopian tourism value chain suggests that local linkages are much stronger than originally thought, particularly outside Addis Ababa (Mitchell and Coles, 2009).

Figure 4.2 *Comparative tourism value chains in Africa: Approximate cost allocation for a 12-day high season package from the UK to various African destinations*

comparable data in this area. Christie and Crompton (2001) emphasize the developmental significance of tourist expenditure outside the hotel, which they report to typically vary widely between half and double in-hotel expenditure. The scale of spending beyond the hotel varies between different countries in part reflecting the different capability of the local economy to supply the goods and services that tourists demand. Out of hotel expenditure in Barbados, Cyprus and Jamaica constitutes 82 per cent, 100–130 per cent and 61 per cent of in-hotel expenditure respectively (Christie and Crompton, 2001).

Evidence from Kenya suggests that spending outside the hotel also varies by the type of tourism. City and coastal tourism results in out of hotel expenditure of 50 per cent of hotel spending, whereas the figure is up to 113 per cent to 188 per cent on safari (Christie and Crompton, 2001).

Interventions to support the informal sector
Policy interventions may either enhance or constrain small and medium enterprises and informal sector opportunities.

Shah and Gupta's review of tourism in Asia (1998) states that the informal sector receives little attention from planners and, as a result of this, often operates within a disenabling environment for enterprise. Studies conducted by

Weru (2007) and Mtui (2007) indicate that in Kenya and Tanzania policy constraints such as multiple taxes, onerous regulations and the lack of access to credit present barriers for the poor to access market opportunities.

In a review of the plan to stimulate economic growth and promote regional development in Senegal, it was found that 'the lack of recognition and legal framework for culture-related occupations leaves them marginalised and part of the informal sector' (Crompton and Christie, 2003, p26). Whilst 'formalization' of the informal sector has to be handled sensitively, to avoid erecting ever-higher barriers to the market for the poor, this does not justify simply marginalizing the informal sector. In Senegal, the youth working in the cultural sector found themselves with irregular income and without access to welfare assistance.

There are also some positive examples of intervention. Kubsa (2007) illustrates how recognition and training of local guides in Ethiopia has helped these micro-entrepreneurs get established. In Yogyakarta, Indonesia, a flexible licensing system, a cooperative and an association assisted vendors to improve their position in the tourism economy (Timothy and Wall, 1997). In Mauritius, Page (1999) highlights the impact of a policy of increasing Mauritian shopping opportunities in significantly reducing the scale of handicraft and souvenir sales that were imported from its high level of 90 per cent in 1988.

Few interventions gather ex-ante and ex-post income data to quantify their impact. One exception is an intervention in The Gambia, funded by the UK Department for International Development (DFID) during 1999–2002. Assisting the informal sector juice sellers, craft makers, local guides and beach 'bumsters' to formalize themselves into properly constituted producer entities, adopt codes of conduct, improve their services, and liaise with hotels, led to substantial increases in small enterprise income. Income increases arising from this initiative ranged from 18 per cent to 33 per cent for the licensed guides, more than doubling income for the juice pressers, and doubling or tripling for craft market vendors (Bah and Goodwin, 2003).

Non-labour income

'Collective income' is the term used to describe pro-poor benefit flows that do not accrue to a single worker, entrepreneur or household, but accrue to a community – in other words, non-labour income.

There are broadly three types of collective income:

- Income earned by community institutions, resulting from their economic stake in a tourism enterprise. These include lease fees and rentals paid for use of community assets, dividends from equity shares and other similar royalties. A slightly different type of income is collective profits from a community-run business. These are known as 'on-project' benefits (Warner, 2005) as they derive from the day-to-day operation of a tourism business.
- Philanthropic flows. These are benefit flows that are not integral to the business operation itself so are termed 'off-project benefits'. They include

donations in cash or kind to a community, from a tourism operator or tourists themselves.
* Shares of protected area fees that are transferred to, or spent on, communities adjacent to protected areas.

Collective income from leases, equity and rentals

There are two distinct models of on-project collective benefit flows, which are both important elements of the pro-poor tourism discourse. The first of these is the experiences of 'joint ventures'[1] between local communities and private sector tourism operators, mainly in southern Africa. The second model is a much broader and more diffuse collection of projects in which communities normally own and operate the tourism assets without the same form of partnership with the private sector. This model of tourist development can be categorized as community-based tourism (CBT).[2]

In parts of Africa, community–private sector 'joint ventures' are common and have been the focus of a number of reviews (Poultney and Spenceley, 2001; Spenceley, 2003; Mahony and Van Zyl, 2001; Massyn and Koch, 2004a; PPT Toolkit Task Team, 2005; Ashley and Jones, 2001). This is particularly the case in southern Africa (particularly South Africa, Namibia and Botswana), where high potential eco-tourism real estate is often owned either communally or by the state.

In order to develop the tourism product in such areas, therefore, the private sector has to gain some form of lease or concession to use the land for a defined time period. In the first decade of democracy in South Africa about 20 of these joint ventures were concluded. There are also joint venture operations in East Africa (Tanzania and Kenya) (Mtui, 2007; Weru, 2007; Hatfield, 2005), the first has just opened in Rwanda (Verdugo, 2007), and interest is being expressed further afield, such as in Egypt and Uganda.[3] The relevance to this review is that these joint venture arrangements may include significant benefit flows to poor communities in addition to wages and contracts that benefit employees and tourist entrepreneurs respectively.

The evidence suggests that the scale of community earnings from joint ventures varies considerably.

As illustrated in Table 4.7, there are joint ventures generating around $95,000 per year for the community while others generate very much less. Some fail and never generate anything (for example, as reported by Kubsa (2007) in Ethiopia and Spenceley (2003) in South Africa and Mozambique). The most positive trend is seen in Namibia, where the number of joint venture lodges in operation, and community income generated from them, have been on a steadily increasing trend for several years.

Reviewing the first generation of joint ventures in southern Africa, Boonzaaier, (2002) summarized the royalties based upon turnover in Namibia, Botswana and South Africa. On average, the joint venture fees negotiated were in the range of 5–10 per cent of lodge turnover.

Joint ventures present practical problems from a poverty reduction perspective. On the negative side, they often require highly complex arrangements

Table 4.7 *Examples of collective income earnings*

		Source
Community income from stake in one lodge	*South Africa* Lekgophung Lodge, Madikwe Game Reserve: $95,000 per annum from concession fees Wilderness Lodge, Makuleke: $59,000 per annum from concession fees	Massyn and Koch, 2004b
	Tanzania Ololosokwan village, western Serengeti: Over $90,000 per annum from fees and jobs	Mtui, 2007
	Zambia Sekute Development Trust: Established 11 contracts with private operators deriving earnings of approximately $2500 per month from the use of facilities within the chiefdom by tourists	Metcalfe, 2005
Overall scale and significance of collective income	*Namibia* Namibian conservancies: In 2005 had 10 joint venture lodges and 12 trophy hunting contracts, increasing total conservancy cash income from $110,000 in 1998 to $1.6 million in 2005 (the bulk from joint venture tourism)	NACSO, 2006
	Four different approaches for spending the money have emerged: • Individual cash payouts to registered members • Payouts to conservancy members in Nyae Nyae conservancy, which in 2002 amounted to 60% of average annual individual income, and payouts to conservancy members in Torra conservancy, which in 2002 amounted to 14% of average annual individual income • Payouts on a village basis, for villages to make allocation decisions • Expenditure on social services such as schools, farmers, pensioners, orphans	
Case studies	*Six international pro-poor tourism case studies (South Africa; Ecuador; Namibia and Uganda; Nepal; and St Lucia)*	
	Collective income equivalent to 4–46% of total local benefits Indirect beneficiaries of 200–26,000 per enterprise compared to direct beneficiaries of 41–120 per enterprise Benefits are from funds spent on education, health care and communication Incomes ranged from $79 to $24,000 per enterprise (micro ventures to partnership lodge) equivalent to income per household of $0.15 to $64 per year	Ashley et al, 2001

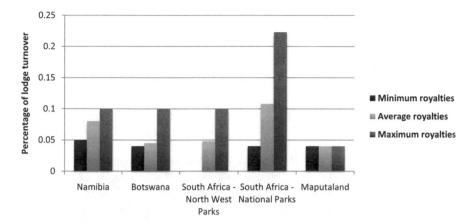

Source: Boonzaaier, 2002

Figure 4.3 *Royalties based on turnover, southern Africa, 2002*

and thus facilitation for their successful implementation and long-term sustainability (PPT Toolkit Task Team, 2005; Metcalfe, 2005; Gujadhur, 2001). This is a real problem because there are a significant number of joint ventures that, as a result of poor design, have greatly reduced benefit flows to the community (Weru, 2007; Mtui, 2007; Spenceley, 2001). In addition, they often generate rather low and volatile returns in the short to medium term for the community. Also, funds that are generated do not always reach poor households in the community.

Nevertheless, joint ventures are a potential benefit pathway for poor rural communities for the following reasons:

- Collective income potentially benefits a much wider range of households than individual income. This is particularly important in poor rural areas in Africa where many of the population are too young, too old or too sick to work. In six international PPT case studies (Ashley et al, 2001), the number of beneficiaries from collective income was 5 to 20 times the number of wage earners.
- Rural communities generally have few collective income-generating options. Whilst collective income flows may be small relative to wage earnings, they are large compared to other communal options, and thus can fund community investments that would not otherwise happen – so can have a major impact on a community investment fund and its membership (Spenceley, 2001; Mulonga and Murphy, 2003; NACSO, 2006).
- Collective income may not be as large as wages, but it can still be a substantial additional benefit flow. In the MAFISA review (Massyn and Koch 2004a) of the concession agreements set up around the Madikwe Game Reserve in the North West Province of South Africa, the most productive joint venture

Box 4.5 *Second generation joint venture structure on the Wild Coast, South Africa*

The diagram below outlines a fairly typical concession arrangement negotiated in 2004 between Wilderness Safaris, a successful high-end South African eco-tourism company and a community trust representing one of the poorest communities in South Africa (on the northern end of the 'Wild Coast' in Eastern Cape Province).[4]

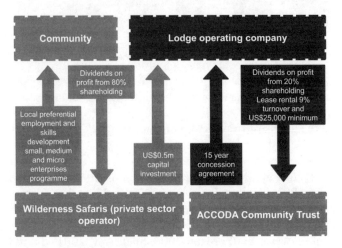

In addition to local employment and procurement, two sources of collective income for the trust were agreed in return for use of the site – a lease (paid as a percentage of turnover over and above a minimum threshold) and a dividend paid on profits (on the basis of equity to purchase an existing lodge structure owned by the community). The proceeds were to be paid into the trust and distributed in line with the democratic constitution of the community-owned and managed legal entity.

generated collective income equivalent to 35 per cent of all local income from the lodge. In other cases it is a smaller boost to local incomes. For example in one partnership lodge at Rocktail Bay in KwaZulu-Natal, the volume of money flowing into this impoverished community in the form of wages is about 15 times larger than the community benefits occurring in the form of community shares (Spenceley, 2001).

• The fact that the community has a legal stake in the enterprise means that it can, under certain circumstances, leverage an increase in other financial benefit flows, aside from the collective cash flow. This is well illustrated at Lekgophung Lodge in South Africa (Massyn and Koch 2004a) where total local earnings are three times higher than in other 'conventional' lodges, and only part of the difference is directly attributable to the joint venture fee (see Box 4.6).

- In addition to cash flows, communities are able to secure non-financial benefits from their partnership. In Namibia, for example, many agreements include the development of non-financial social infrastructure, such as local schools, sports and soup kitchens (NACSO, 2006).
- In order to establish a joint venture, a community must form itself into a legal entity. This process can be time consuming but can have substantial knock-on effects by creating a legitimate legal body for interaction with government, the private sector, formal markets and the legal system. For example in Zambia, the Sekute Community Trust was originally formed to facilitate tourism development. However, the Trust was sufficiently strong to successfully challenge an investor who had illegally taken a prime island site on the Zambezi (Metcalfe, 2005). Namibian conservancies are beginning to change the way that decision making and representation takes place (NACSO, 2006).
- Reduce the financial volatility that plagues many poor rural households.

Several factors appear to determine the size and distribution of collective income from rents, royalties and dividends:

- The cohesion of the host community and the transparency with which collective income is distributed (Spenceley 2001, 2003). There are many examples of 'community' income being left in a bank account or misused. (PPT Toolkit Task Team, 2005) However, there are also examples of consultative community decisions to use funds for productive local

---

Box 4.6 *Examples of community stake being used to leverage additional benefits*

At Lekgophong Lodge, in Madikwe Game Reserve in South Africa, the community has the long-term lease to the lodge site, and holds equity in the Lodge development company. It earns around $94,000 per year in concession fees, which represents an additional 50 per cent on top of local wage earnings. What is noticeable is that wage and small enterprise earnings are also higher at Lekgophung than at other private lodges in Madikwe, due to the community's stronger bargaining power. Total local earnings per bed are nearly three times higher than at the other lodges.

Damaraland Camp in northwest Namibia operates on a site leased from the Torra Conservancy. The community used the negotiation process to secure a range of benefits in addition to its 10 per cent of camp revenue. These included commitments to training, and a shift from revenue shares to transfer of equity in years 10 to 15 of the contract (Ashley and Jones, 2001).

investments, such as a cattle dip, or cash distributions to households (Mulonga and Murphy, 2003; Ashley et al, 2001).
- The legal, financial and technical design of the partnership between the private sector and the community, and the nature of the concession contract (PPT Toolkit Task Team, 2005).
- The capacity of the community to understand and assert their legal rights and assets (Mtui, 2007; Weru, 2007; Kubsa, 2007).
- The time lag before significant collective income starts to flow after signing the agreement. This depends on the extent of community asset ownership – whether it is limited to land and natural resource or includes a stake in the operating company. If commercial assets have been secured by the community, the way in which these have been financed (loan or grant) impacts directly on payback periods (PPT Toolkit Task Team, 2005).
- The viability of the project itself will influence the flow of collective income. Wilderness Safaris had two joint ventures in KwaZulu-Natal in South Africa. One at Rocktail Bay is expanding, with a new diving site and additional joint venture currently under development, while the other lodge in Ndumo Game Reserve failed commercially and the developer, Wilderness Safaris, closed the lodge – with the result that community benefit flows ceased (Ashley, 2005).

As Mtui (2007) comments with respect to Tanzania, 'Joint ventures can generate high returns but be painstakingly difficult to transparently negotiate and manage.' The main constraint for joint venture income flows are the 'unfair distribution of benefits from community business ventures due to lack of business, legal, bargaining and contractual comprehension by local people.'

Community-based tourism (CBT)

CBT is a quite different approach to generating collective income compared with the community–private sector 'joint ventures' discussed above. CBT is an umbrella term – the central tenets normally involve communities fully owning and operating tourism facilities. This implies either no role, or a very circumscribed one, for the private sector. CBT is often supported by NGOs and external donors as an explicit attempt to develop an 'alternative' tourism, with greater benefits reaching the poor (Halstead, 2003; Clauzel, 2005; Rozemeijer et al, 2001; Murphy and Halstead, 2003; Mulonga and Murphy, 2003; Hainsworth, 2006; Williams et al, 2001). Some CBT successfully results in many individuals earning income, from dancing, pottery, campsite attendance, guiding, crafting etc. While such earnings fall under the MSE category already covered above, practitioners generally consider both collective and individual earnings for a specific community together.

CBT earnings tend to be modest relative to the investment costs for tourist facilities, but advocates suggest they generate income that is useful at household or community level as well as other livelihood benefits. Halstead's assessment of community-based tourism in the Caprivi region of Namibia found campsite workers earning around $516 per year, and craft workers earning even less (Halstead, 2003). Non-financial benefits are also highlighted in the livelihood and enterprise analysis done. For example, Murphy and Halstead (2003) emphasize the training and enterprise skills, which have enabled some individuals to move on to better jobs. Although some CBT organizations collapse during periods of low demand, some later evolve and re-emerge.

The capacity of most CBT projects to generate sustainable profits varies, generally around a low level. In Caprivi, the indications are that many community-owned tourism enterprises are not currently financially viable, although the authors remain steadfastly optimistic about the future prospects of profitability (Murphy and Halstead, 2003). Other analyses assert the financial viability of CBT enterprises (Barnes et al, 2001; Diggle, 2003). However, financial viability is the Achilles heel of CBT projects. Bond's (2001) assessment of the CAMPFIRE programme in Zimbabwe, a cause celebre for many advocates of CBT, is damning: 'current examples of community-based tourism or non-lease tourism have proved not to be financially viable and seem unlikely to drive processes of institutional change'. A recent analysis of CBT in Namibia (Hitchins and Highstead, 2005) reported that only one-third of CBT organizations were operating above break-even point.

There is very little information in the CBT literature on how poor the intended beneficiaries of projects are. CBT as a model is generally applied by donors and NGOs in rural areas, often areas with wilderness resources but a lack of other economic options. The economic status of beneficiaries is generally considered to be low on the basis of assumption, rather than assessment. There is also little analysis of the relative position, within their community, of those who operate the CBT enterprises. This appears, at times, to be based on the generally unrealistic assumption of social homogeneity in African villages that is surprisingly widespread amongst some in the development sector.

There are two opposing views on the significance of CBT. On the one hand, analyses focused on livelihoods of the poor find that, even where the financial success of projects has been limited, the benefits are meaningful to poor households in remote areas (Murphy and Halstead, 2003). To those that get access to benefits, they are important, even if they are meagre and unsustainable. It has been argued that CBT should be seen merely as providing a complementary source of income or livelihoods to supplement already existing livelihoods (Kiyiapi et al, 2005).

On the other hand, there is growing scepticism of the value of CBT in delivering poverty reduction because of the inability of most schemes to achieve their most fundamental goal, of directing sustainable and meaningful benefit flows to poor communities. The profusion of unsustainable, supply-side CBT projects attests to this, and many donor-funded projects 'disappear' after funding cycles end (Epler-Wood, 2004). In the EU-funded 12.9 million Wild Coast Spatial Development Initiative Programme, the mid-term review found that revenue from community projects was just 2 per cent of the target (European Commission, 2003).

While recognizing hard-won social gains for participants in Namibia, Hitchins and Highstead (2005) suggest that CBT-supported interventions are not adequately stimulating locally provided services, nor facilitating a conducive business environment. They thus create dependency and perpetuate exclusion from the mainstream tourism market. CBT is charged with inflating expectations about what tourism can reasonably deliver to poor communities and then failing to deliver them by developing inappropriate tourist product in the wrong places, managed by inexperienced people with confused objectives. The key determinant of their success is proximity to established tourism routes and links to the mainstream private sector – an approach often overlooked when social development and business development objectives are conflated.

A detailed appraisal of CBT in Zambia (Dixey, 2005, see also Box 4.7) closely echoes the Namibia study. CBT is generally ineffective at providing a significant flow of finance to the supposed beneficiaries. Dixey also corroborates the factors that are more likely to generate a meaningful pro-poor impact, namely a close linkage to the private sector and to tourists themselves.

Box 4.7 *Findings from CBT appraisals in Namibia and Zambia*

An assessment of CBT interventions in Namibia concluded:

> *The reality is that for many areas and communities prospects for tourism appear to be marginal, in the face of a less attractive tourism product and a myriad of deep-seated constraints, such as geographic remoteness from tourism routes, access to water, electricity, telecommunications and transport. The activity that has occurred in these areas is due to high levels of support from development agencies. In terms of net welfare gained or the sustainability of outcomes it is valid to at least question the efficacy of such intensive levels of support* (Hitchins and Highstead, 2005, p17).

In attempting to introduce rural communities to tourism value chains, agencies are taking extremely underdeveloped communities and trying to link them to a modern, sophisticated export-oriented service industry. Agencies are forced to make very high levels of investment in social and community development in order simply to get to a point where a small proportion of more capable members of the community, in the right locations, can contemplate starting a tourism-related business. In doing so the distinction between social development and business development are often blurred.

A recent economic analysis in Namibia compares the financial cost of all interventions in community-based natural resource management with the economic benefit of the programme, and finds a positive rate of return on the investment (Barnes et al, 2001). This is still consistent with the reality of small struggling CBT enterprises, as joint venture lodge income and the value of increased wildlife stocks constitute the major items of economic return. In other words, the actual beneficiaries of CBT are often non-poor tourism operators and wildlife – rather than the local communities in whose name these projects are justified and resources mobilized.

An appraisal of CBT enterprises in Zambia concluded:

> *A few CBT projects have failed and many will struggle to be profitable resulting in disillusioned communities. The main reason for this is that much CBT has been inappropriately donor-driven not market-led. CBT has performed poorly due to multiple and conflicting objectives and vested interests, a lack of market research, weak linkages to the tourism industry, small marketing profile, low product quality and development levels in communities, internal community disputes and poor local governance, and a lack of information dissemination, coordination and planning and sharing of common lessons and good practice* (Dixey, 2005, p65).

> *CBT has been most successful when it has been private sector driven ensuring commercial viability. Several tourism companies advise and promote highly successful CBT enterprises as a high proportion of tourists are interested in community and cultural activities* (Dixey, 2005, p65).

> *A combination of factors that show a strong positive correlation with success are: Market linkages to tourism companies; proximity to the tourism market; competitive advantage; financial management; visitor handling; and, community motivation. Factors that show a slight positive correlation with success are: product quality and community investment. External investment (donor funding) has a very strong negative correlation with success. This is a result of inappropriate donor interventions and does not necessarily mean that external assistance cannot be effective* (Dixey, 2005, p50).

These findings are repeated across the African continent, from East Africa (Hatfield, 2005) to southern Africa (Spenceley, 2008). In a study on the nexus between tourism development, conservation and sustainability, Hawkins et al (2002) concluded that while many NGOs and donor agencies have worked with communities to develop tourism, the resulting initiatives have often been supply rather than demand-based and have not involved the private sector. As a consequence, their sustainability is questionable.

In the light of these findings, the fact that several external donors have focused support in the tourism sector largely on community-based tourism is surprising. The paradox is that development assistance is being applied to finance projects that are largely ineffective at benefiting the poor, in part because of the involvement of donors themselves. The notion of boosting market access for communities to engage in the tourism sector can be sound in a limited number of places, where there is a genuine commercial possibility of success. Many failed CBT projects have their inception in the flawed logic of an approach which suggests 'there is nothing else to do in this remote place, so let's try tourism and see if it helps conservation too' (Goodwin, 2006b, 2006c; Dixey, 2005; Crompton and Christie, 2003). In those places where community-based tourism does have a chance of success, it is clear that the more market-oriented model outlined is the path to success. Let us see more comparative research between CBT projects and private sector projects in the same place, to understand their similarities and differences – but also their interdependencies (for an excellent example see Harrison and Schipani, 2007).

Philanthropic flows to communities

There are many different types of philanthropic flows from the tourism sector to poor communities. Many accommodation establishments, particularly in rural areas, donate funds, or equipment, to local projects. Some hotels, lodges and tour operators collect donations from their guests. There is also the merging of tourism and voluntary development work, with organizations that arrange for tourists to work on a community project. Many tour companies, concerned about the transparency of public sector bureaucracies in tourist destinations in developing countries, make donations to local or international NGOs to manage corporate donations (UNEP, 2005).

An active CSR programme can boost local earnings from a lodge or hotel. For example, two Conservation Corporation Africa lodges in South Africa illustrate the volume of philanthropic funds that can be generated from high-end niche tourism products (Massyn and Koch, 2004b). In these lodges, philanthropic flows amounted to tens of thousands of dollars per year. A recent study in Livingstone in Zambia found that almost two-thirds of tourism enterprises contributed to social and community activities in 2005, contributing on average nearly $3000 (DCDM Consulting, 2006).

The beneficiaries of philanthropic flows are generally in the immediate vicinity of tourism operations. While there is likely to be some elite capture of benefits, the investments can also be targeted at those not economically active, including school children, orphans and the disabled. In this way philanthropic donations can reach those who cannot otherwise participate in the tourism economy.

Commercial drivers in the tourism sector mean it is particularly well suited to boosting philanthropic flows to the poor and this can have a significant pro-poor impact (Meyer, 2006). Firstly, there are obvious commercial benefits to be gained from CSR action, which are specific to tourism given the location and type of client. The added satisfaction that customers have from learning about, or visiting, local projects contributes to the tourist experience. In addition,

Box 4.8 *Community investments from philanthropic donation*

In Maputaland (in northern KwaZulu-Natal, South Africa), an active CSR pro-gramme at Phinda led the Conservation Corporation Africa (CCA) Lodge to out-perform the two other (smaller) lodges in their total local benefit generated, including those with a community equity stake. Local benefit from 'secondary enterprise', including CSR spending, at Phinda amounted to $70,000 per year compared to just $11,000 at other lodges. This represented a 25 per cent boost on top of local employment wages, and thus accounted for 20 per cent of total local benefit (Massyn and Koch, 2004a).

In explaining the unusually high performance at Phinda, the authors point 'to the presence of a dedicated champion in the Phinda operation, who has been responsible for much of the vigour of the CCA's local benefit programme in that region. The disparity between Phinda and elsewhere demonstrates the extent to which local benefit yields in social responsibility models – operating outside a rights-based bargaining arena – depend on the activities of dedicated individuals' (Massyn and Koch, 2004a, p123).

Donations are also often linked with community tourism programmes. For example, in Tanzania, products in the Cultural Tourism Programme are structured so that the tour fee includes a contribution to the Village Development Fund. The VDF funds community development initiatives such as education (classrooms, books, desks), water supply, health services (dispensary rooms, maternity wards). Tourists are able to make further donations to the projects they visit. Between 2002 and 2005, donations amounted to $11,700 in one location (Mto-wa-Mbu) and this amounted to 13 per cent of total local incomes from cultural tours in that period (Mtui, 2007).

tourism operators in developing countries often need local 'social' licences to operate (Goodwin, 2006b; Ashley et al, 2005).

There are added incentives to invest in CSR in places where the industry is under pressure to increase the empowerment of the poor. In South Africa, for instance, the tourist sector has agreed a sector charter – which commits the industry to a wide range of empowerment objectives aimed at de-racializing the sector – meaning changing the virtual monopoly of white ownership of tourism assets inherited from the Apartheid era (DEAT, 2005). Making significant progress towards the targets agreed in the charter is regarded as preferable to the imposition of empowerment targets by government.

Tourists themselves are a large potential source of charitable donations. Accommodation establishments have an opportunity to facilitate significant off-project benefits at the destination that are financed by someone else (Meyer, 2006; Ashley et al, 2005). The role of hoteliers or tour operators can be to establish the institutional conduit that allows tourists to make donations with a good degree of confidence that the funds will be managed transparently and contribute effectively to community development. In Livingstone, Zambia, of the $2000 contributed from the accommodation sector to be spent on community and social activities in 2005, 90 per cent was from guests (DCDM Consulting, 2006).

The benefit accruing to the communities concerned varies. There are positive examples where livelihoods have been dramatically improved through initiatives such as eye clinics to perform cataract operations (Harrison, 2004) and others where initiatives have been much less successful (Spenceley, 2003).

The pro-poor tourism literature suggests that, while the benefits from philanthropy can have an important positive impact on local livelihoods, the greater challenge is to adapt business practice to make greater use of local labour, products and services (Ashley and Haysom, 2006; Mitchell and Ashley, 2008). In much of the tourism industry, discussion on social responsibility focuses heavily on philanthropy rather than harnessing the development potential of the core business. For example, the vast majority of 'flagship' CSR interventions listed by the World Tourism and Travel Council appear to be off-project – entirely separate from the day-to-day business – rather than involving adaptations to how business is done (for example, WTTC, 2002).

The Spier Resort in South Africa has a long record of local philanthropic investment on a multitude of initiatives. However, the scale of these benefits was dwarfed by the gains from adapting procedures to increase procurement from historically disadvantaged local suppliers. However, this will not always be the case. UNEP outlines a broad range of tourist initiatives that have raised significant resources for community and environmental causes (UNEP, 2005).

In several African countries, governments have instituted mechanisms to directly allocate a percentage of entry fees to parks and reserves to neighbouring communities. Often the funds are invested in local projects, rather than distributed in the form of cash.

In Kenya, local governments allocate approximately 19 per cent of tourism revenues to the local communities neighbouring the local protected areas – including Maasai Mara National Reserve, Lake Bogoria National Reserve and Samburu National Reserve. In contrast, park fees collected by the Kenya Wildlife Service are partially re-invested in the form of community projects through its Community Service department (Weru, 2007).

In Tanzania, the share of revenue collected from park fees which is re-invested in the local community is a highly political and contested issue and one in which public authorities are far from transparent. It is claimed that shares ranging from 7.5 per cent to 25 per cent of total fees accruing to the Tanzanian National Parks Authority from tourism and hunting activities are channelled back to the surrounding local communities in the form of development projects such as school and health buildings, bridges, water supply and training (Mtui, 2007). In the Ngorongoro Conservation Area Authority[5] about $1.2 million is disbursed to the Pastoral Council whose role is to represent the local community.

Recent fieldwork has suggested that the shares of park revenue that are distributed to local communities are much smaller than often claimed by the public authorities (often only amounting to about 5 per cent of park fees) and there is anecdotal evidence of serious governance issues relating to the disbursement of funds through the Pastoral Council. These findings were subject to a public consultation process in Tanzania in late 2008 and were not challenged by a broad range of tourism stakeholders (Mitchell et al, 2009).

In Rwanda national parks, a new revenue sharing scheme was initiated in 2005. Revenue sharing of 5 per cent of gross park receipts has been implemented in all three national parks and the share is distributed to local residents throughout the district (Verdugo, 2007).

However, several authors identify obstacles to the funds actually reaching communities, especially when they have to pass through several layers of bureaucracy from Treasury to district and village level. As Mtui (2007, p24) states 'many villages do not receive these funds at all, or receive it too late and too little'.

If funds reach communities, they have the potential to reach a wide range of the population, including those who are not economically active. In such remote communities, the funds could be a substantial addition, although there is limited scope for long-term increase given the trade-off that protected area authorities face in keeping fees to fund their own operations.

Non-financial impacts on livelihoods

We sometimes overlook the self-evident fact that poverty is not only a result of lack of income. It therefore follows that the direct effects of tourism on the poor go well beyond cash flows. This review is focused on economic, rather than social or cultural, impacts on the poor. This, however, does not preclude exploration of the many non-financial impacts that directly affect livelihoods and poverty levels.

Access to natural assets, such as grazing rights, fish stocks or livelihood options that buffer a household against risk, can be as influential on poverty levels as a flow of cash income. Some of the direct effects noted in the literature have a considerable overlap with the dynamic changes in the economy as these will lead to changes in the livelihood assets and options of poor households. These effects impact most significantly on households living in and around tourism destinations, and are not limited to those who participate economically in tourism.

Some of the most commonly identified impacts from the tourism sector are:

- changes in access to services and infrastructure (e.g. health care, transport, radio/satellite communication, competition for water);
- changes in access to natural resources, such as land, grazing, coastline, marine resources;
- access to new contacts and networks, usable for other livelihood activities;
- understanding of, and increased access to, markets;
- language skills and other service skills;

- community organization, evidenced by the creation of formal institutional structures for managing tourism inputs or revenues;
- a stimulus to other ongoing reforms, such as in land restitution, natural resource management, or land planning.

Table 4.8 illustrates a wide variety of livelihood impacts experienced by local communities in a number of different tourism destinations.

Positive impacts on non-cash livelihoods are noted in the literature though rarely with any attempt at quantification (Murphy and Halstead, 2003; Nicanor, 2001; Bramman and Fundación Acción Amazonia, 2001; Jamieson et al, 2004; Ashley, 2000). Weru (2007) gives examples of lodges in remote areas assisting locals by providing basic services such as water, and health services. Tortilis Camp in the Amboseli Region of Kenya has assigned specific times of the day when locals can go to fetch water from its borehole. Keekorok Lodge's clinic sometimes handles health emergency cases from the neighbouring communities.

Much of the evidence comes from micro-level and anecdotal case studies. More detail exists on the negative impacts experienced by poor households from tourism, particularly in relation to lost access to natural resources or the opportunity cost of resources used for tourism and conservation. Slob and Wilde-Ramsing (2006) cite an ILO study of tourism investment resulting in the eviction of Maasai from traditional grounds in Tanzania and fishermen evicted from the Kerala coasts to make way for large tourist complexes.

Detailed anthropological and ecological work has highlighted negative livelihood impacts on pastoralists in Tanzania (Homewood and Brockington, 1999). Dina (cited in Goodwin, 2006a) reports how the fishing activities of the Bedouin were negatively affected as a result of hotel expansion along the south Sinai coast. Sutton et al (2004) found that the cost of wildlife damage on the local agriculture in east Caprivi accounts for 6 per cent of annual household income. He suggests that a scheme should be formulated to compensate local farmers for the crop damage they suffer as a result of wildlife – and to provide a financial incentive for farmers to refrain from destroying the animals that are harming their livelihoods but on which the tourism industry depends. Hatfield and Malleret-King (2007) estimate that the opportunity costs of not farming the Bwindi and Virunga gorilla mountain forests in Uganda amount to about $13 million per year (on the basis of output foregone, assuming 50 per cent of the park area would be cultivable) – which is considerably higher than the $1 million or so earnt annually by local people from gorilla tourism.

Those affected by livelihood change are likely to be in the direct vicinity of tourism operations, Negative effects are most likely to accrue to those who are reliant on natural resources, such as grazing or marine life. In understanding the significance of livelihood changes the distribution of effects is as important as the scale. This is particularly so when there are livelihood losses, because the losers are often different from the beneficiaries. For example in Caprivi, Namibia, both O'Connell (1995) and Sutton et al (2004) estimate total agricultural losses due to wildlife to be lower than the aggregate local income from

Table 4.8 *Key non-financial livelihood impacts noted in seven international case studies*

	SNV Nepal	Tropical Ecuador	NACOBTA Namibia	UCOTA Uganda	SDI/PPP South Africa	Wilderness South Africa	St Lucia HTP St Lucia
Positive	Enhanced community organization, mobilization and participation in local government and NGOs	An 'outside friend' for information, advice and connections	Jobs, market opportunities and income reduce hunger and vulnerability	Business opportunities, skills and market access reduce vulnerability	Land restitution is main source of impacts so far	Increased contact and exposure (information, catalyst of ideas)	Giving value to popular culture
	More opportunities for micro-enterprise	Communication (donated radio, use of phone and transport) mitigates remoteness	Community income for local priorities, e.g. church toilet, funerals, schools, internet	Community income and organization, especially for education and health	Tourism further stimulates community organization and determination	Infrastructural improvements in remote areas (malaria control, roads, power)	Development of an alternative and optimism in the face of banana sector decline
	Health/transport and infrastructure improvements related to tourism	Can use contacts to pursue land claims, generate international support, influence policy	Training, improved skills	A focus for further support from donors and tourists	Injection of donor funds, particularly for training and capacity building	Income (substantial for workers, high degree re-spent locally)	Geographic dispersion of jobs and enterprise opportunities; enterprise support
	Increased awareness of options	Enjoyable contact with tourists, reinforces pride and cultural cohesion	Stronger and consultative community organization	Communication and access to information in remote areas		Community funds	Institution-building; development of participatory processes
			A voice at policy level, recognition				
Negative	Poor are exploited – low wages, high commissions	Possible risk of dependence on Tropical	Pressure on natural resources	Pressure on natural resources.	Dependence of community organization on external assistance	Community pride and organization is undermined	Criminality: car theft
	Poor, women, landless are more difficult to include in community organizations and decision making	Opportunity cost of rejecting oil development	Intra-community tension				Problems in community management of collective resources

Note: This aims to illustrate the key types of impact, not their scale of distribution. The case studies report a myriad of mainly positive impacts – these have been prioritized by the case study authors and the authors of this report based on the available evidence, and not by the poor themselves.

Source: Ashley et al, 2001

tourism – so the net effect of tourism is positive for the local economy. The problem is that the negative effects can devastate the livelihood of the specific households concerned, and these households may not have access to any of the benefits of tourism.

Notes

1 The inverted commas signal that there does not have to be joint ownership of equity as in the commercial definition of joint ventures.
2 The term CBT is used in different ways by different people. CBT is often used to refer broadly to small enterprises in a (usually rural) community, even if run by an entrepreneur. Here, such individual businesses fall under MSEs, and CBT relates only to those operated by a community. The term CBT can also be used to include joint ventures. But as there is such a substantive difference between a community-run venture, such as a campsite, and a commercial venture, such as a lodge, in which a community has a stake, we prefer to distinguish them: one as 'joint ventures' and the other as 'CBT'.
3 Ugandan tourism policy explicitly supports concessions with partnerships.
4 The commercial details of the concession are included because they illustrate the sophistication of the 'second generation' joint venture arrangements in southern Africa – which learned from earlier mistakes. Also the concession agreement was abandoned on the point of finalization due to conflicts within the community, so no commercial confidentialities apply.
5 The Ngorongoro Conservation Area Authority was established to manage the Ngorongoro Crater, a multiple-use conservation area that would accommodate both the existing Maasai pastoralists and tourists.

5

Pathway 2: Secondary Benefit Flows from Tourism to the Poor

Why pro-poor secondary flows are important but difficult to assess

Emerging findings suggest that earnings to the poor from tourism expenditure often accrue to people who are not to be found in the 'tourism sector' of the economy – people working in hotels, restaurants, guides or transport. In fact, inter-sectoral linkages can be at least as important as earnings from participation in tourism businesses in some tourist destinations. There is also often scope to increase incomes of the poor from supply chains. It is thus evident that these indirect pro-poor flows are important to assess, and important for policy makers to address.

However, understanding the poverty significance and determinants of indirect incomes to the poor is hampered by three factors. First, a huge economics literature assessing the scale of inter-sectoral linkages in the economy focuses on the scale of those impacts, but often without a distributional focus that is obviously relevant in pro-poor analysis.

Second, the pro-poor tourism (PPT) literature has typically paid scant attention to earnings of the poor from supply chains, compared to the focus on direct participation of the poor in accommodation and guiding services. Third, any discussion of the pro-poor significance of inter-sectoral linkages with tourism can quickly get bogged down in a definitional quagmire regarding terms like 'multipliers', 'linkages' and 'leakages'.

Nevertheless, it is clear from analyses of inter-sectoral impacts, that the indirect impacts of tourism are often considerable, and frequently the participation of the poor is significant but under-researched.

This chapter summarizes what is known about:

- the typical scale of indirect impacts of tourism in the economy;
- the flows reaching the poor from indirect impacts;
- factors affecting the scale or distribution of indirect impacts.

Here the term 'indirect' is used to cover flows between tourism and non-tourism sectors, which can generally refer to backward linkages in the supply chain (see Box 5.1 below). Another type of secondary impact is 'induced' impact. This stems from workers in tourism or tourism supply chains re-spending their earnings and generating further impact. This is also covered in this section, albeit briefly given the dearth of data.

Box 5.1 *Distinguishing direct and indirect benefit flows*

Distinguishing between 'direct' and 'indirect' earnings from tourism should be simple. But it is not. Different authors and methods define this distinction differently. The basic distinction is between activity in the 'tourism sector' and economic activity in the 'non-tourism sector' that is a result of tourist expenditure. The latter is the 'indirect effect'.

The distinction is sometimes described as being between 'first round' expenditure by tourists themselves, and 'second round' expenditure by tourism companies on procuring goods and services from the supply chain on behalf of tourists. This distinction is based on who spends the money rather than the sector of the economy from which goods and services originate. Goods purchased directly by tourists could be non-tourism goods (e.g. shampoo or craft), while goods procured by a hotel could be from the tourism sector (e.g. a tour or an airport transfer).

To make things worse, sometimes analysts use the first round/second round distinction, but then use methods based on a sectoral distinction, like input–output tables (Lejárraga and Walkenhorst, 2006; Kweka et al, 2003). There is a tendency to contrast first round 'direct' earnings from face-to-face tourism services with second round indirect earnings from the 'supply chain' that is more common in micro-level analyses. This distinction is not based on standard economic terms and methods, but more on the experiences of the poor on the ground and whether they interact directly with tourists.

Authors define the 'tourism sector' in different ways, which inevitably impacts on what activities are 'indirect'. Multiplier analysis by Kweka et al (2003) for Tanzania uses the narrow definition of tourism as including activities in hotels and restaurants. The WTTC's satellite accounts take a very broad view of what constitutes 'tourism' – which implies a very narrow view of 'indirect' effects. Most analyses fall between these two polar extremes.

In the end, what matters is to capture all the different ways in which the poor participate in tourism, no matter how they are classified. However, because much PPT research has not paid significant attention to earnings via supply chains, it is important to hang onto the concepts of both direct and indirect impacts, so that both are addressed and neither is forgotten.

What is known about the scale of indirect and induced impacts of tourism?

Indirect impacts

Indications of the scale of indirect impacts (at the macro-economic level although not necessarily for the poor) relative to direct impacts come mainly from several input–output macro-analyses of tourism economies in developing countries. In addition there are a few more recent and detailed destination-level analyses using SAMs or CGE models, and employment estimates for direct and indirect tourism jobs in several countries.

There is also a small literature specifically on agricultural–tourism linkages, of which a major part is food supply. These works help indicate the considerable scale of inter-sectoral linkages between tourism and agriculture. Even though they do not necessarily disaggregate the distribution of benefits to the poor, the findings are significant from a pro-poor perspective because the primary production of much of the food may come from poor households.

An extensive economic impact literature is devoted to quantifying the total economic contribution of tourism to the national economy by using input–output analysis to assess inter-sectoral linkages. These indirect effects are then added to direct effects to reveal the total economic contribution in countries such as Tanzania, Hong Kong, Seychelles, Singapore, Kenya, China and Egypt (see Lin and Sung, 1984; Summary (1987); Fletcher, 1989; Heng and Low, 1990; Kweka et al, 2003; Fan and Oosterhaven, 2005).

These studies suggest that tourism's indirect contribution to the economy ranges between 60 and 120 per cent of direct effects. So, indirect effects may range from half to larger than the direct impacts of tourism. Put another way, the 'ratio multiplier', which simply expresses combined direct and indirect effects, as a proportion of direct effects, tends to fluctuate between 1.6 and 2.2 (it is important not to confuse this ratio multiplier with Keynesian multipliers, which are invariably below 1, and are calculated quite differently – see Box 5.2).

A cross-country analysis of WTTC data produces results that corroborate this finding. The analysis of WTTC's TSA dataset by Lejárraga and Walkenhorst, (2006) finds that the ratio of indirect to direct impact averages 66 per cent in low-income countries and 77 per cent in lower middle-income countries. The only region where the indirect contribution of tourism actually outweighs the direct effect is Europe and Central Asia.

As an example, in Kenya, Summary (1987) reports that the ratio or output multiplier improved between 1971 and 1976, growing from 1.58 to 1.81 as linkages between tourism and agriculture improved. At the same time, the income or Keynesian multiplier worsened from 0.75 to 0.64. Income generated per tourist dollar spent declined.

To add to the confusion, there are also employment multipliers that indicate the amount of employment generated by a unit of tourism expenditure. However, as the denominator is often not clarified and can vary (jobs per thousand South African Rand of tourist expenditure, per thousand dollars etc.), the multiplier figures for different countries are not readily comparable.

Box 5.2 *Muddle on multipliers*

One common way of expressing the relative size of direct and indirect impacts is through the 'ratio multiplier' sometimes also called the 'output' multiplier. The ratio multiplier is:

Indirect contribution of tourism to GDP
Direct plus indirect contribution of tourism to GDP

Thus the ratio multiplier is always over 1 and generally between 1 and 2. As Archer pointed out in 1984 (Archer, 1984) the ratio multiplier says nothing about the expenditure required to cause an economic effect. It just shows the ratio between direct and indirect impacts.

The ratio multiplier should not be confused with the Keynesian multiplier. The Keynesian multiplier measures the amount of income generated in the economy by an additional unit of tourist expenditure and is defined as:

Contribution of tourism to the economy (direct plus indirect)
Tourist expenditure

This measures something entirely different to the ratio multiplier, i.e. the economic impacts resulting from a unit of tourist expenditure.

Also, sometimes estimates may appear to corroborate each other, when in fact this is because findings or assumptions are shared between different pieces of research. Preliminary TSAs may be undertaken in countries with insufficient data by using ratios from other countries. Much analysis depends on ratios embedded within a country's input–output tables, but these again may depend on unfounded assumptions or ratios that have been borrowed from elsewhere.

In Turpie et al's (2006) analysis of Namibian tourism, and Blake et al's (2008) analysis of Brazilian tourism (both of which draw on input–output tables for their more detailed SAMs or CGE models) indirect impacts are equivalent to 86 per cent and 63 per cent of direct impacts respectively.

Some of the input–output studies find that the inter-sectoral linkages from tourism are higher than for other sectors. For example, Kweka et al (2003), find that tourism (hotels and restaurants only) generates a high demand for output of other sectors in Tanzania. The output multiplier is estimated to be 1.8, meaning a $1m increase in tourism output stimulates the whole economy to expand by $1.8m. This multiplier is higher than the equivalent estimates for agriculture, manufacturing and other services. Particularly significant backward linkages are food and beverages, fishing and hunting, and wholesale and retail trade. Similarly in Senegal, a 1996 study cited in Crompton and Christie (2003) found that tourism (defined as hotels, bars and restaurants) consumed more local inputs than any other sector. However, when making

---

Box 5.3 *Recognizing indirect impacts*

In Kenya, the Ministry of Tourism and Wildlife surveyed a Kenyan tourist beach and recognized only four kinds of informal enterprise – craft sellers, boat operators, safari sellers and fishermen. In 2006, a more thorough assessment – which was part of a beach management initiative – revealed entrepreneurs engaged in a multitude of activities that had not been previously recognized. Enterprises were selling food, miscellaneous goods, massages, equipment rental and commercial sex, and working as money changers, translators and photographers (Liaison Development Consultants, 2006).

---

comparisons with other sectors, it must be noted that these studies use narrow definitions of tourism (accommodation, bars and restaurants), so much tourist-related activity that actually falls within the tourism sector (e.g. transportation) will appear here as an inter-sectoral linkage – when it is actually a linkage within the tourist sector.

Another source of data on indirect effects comes from estimates of total tourism-related employment compared to direct tourism employment. These suggest that indirect impacts are considerable, and sometimes greatly exceed direct impacts. In the Seychelles, Archer and Fletcher (1996) estimated that secondary employment generated by tourism slightly exceeded direct employment in tourism (4540 indirect jobs compared to 3772 direct jobs). Christie and Crompton (2001) report that Mauritius had some 16,500 people working directly in hotels, restaurants, and travel and tourism – but almost twice as many (some 30,000) working in indirect jobs. Spending outside the hotel generates growth of domestic industries in agriculture, fishing, food processing, construction, furniture making and handicrafts. In Senegal, the indirect jobs are estimated to be one and a half times the direct jobs in tourism – 18,000 indirect jobs compared with 12,000 direct jobs (Crompton and Christie, 2003). In Tanzania, indirect jobs were estimated to be more than double direct tourism jobs in 1992 (117,000 compared to 53,000) (Kweka et al, 2003). Some estimates compare hotel jobs (only) to total tourism jobs. In Tunisia, total tourism-related employment is estimated to be roughly three times the number of hotel jobs (UNCTAD, 2007).

While there is significant variation in employment estimates by destination and definition, the general picture is that indirect employment is estimated to be greater than direct employment, with the range being that indirect employment can be from a half to double the figures for direct employment.

Thus the broad picture that emerges from across the data is that indirect inter-sectoral linkages are likely to boost the economic impacts of tourism by more than 50 per cent, on top of the direct impacts. In most developing countries, an extra 60 per cent to 80 per cent seems likely and in some the boost appears even higher. Thus if the distribution of these flows follows a

Table 5.1 *Evidence of the scale and significance of inter-sectoral linkages*

Additional GDP output from indirect linkages (i.e. GDP increase from non-tourism sectors resulting from a unit increase in tourism output)

National studies using input–output analysis (including SAMs and CGE models)	Brazil +63%	Blake et al, 2008
	Namibia (Protected Areas) +86%	Turpie et al, 2004
	Tanzania: +83%	Kweka et al, 2003
Cross country regression of TSA data (also using input–output tables	Africa: +59%	Lejárraga and
	South Asia: +52%	Walkenhorst 2006
	East Asia & Pacific: +78%	

similar pattern to the distribution of direct tourism flows (discussed below), they are clearly significant as a potential source of a third to a half of all pro-poor earnings.

Induced impacts

Secondary impacts are usually defined as a combination of indirect effects (via non-tourism sectors) and induced effects (via tourism workers spending their wages). As wages are re-spent, this can in turn create new income-earning opportunities for poor people, just as the tourism supply chain can (depending of course on who is spending what and how). Type II multiplier estimates include induced effects. However, there are generally little data specifically on the scale of induced effects. One such source is Heng and Low's (1990) analysis of Singapore. As shown in Table 5.2, the induced effect is estimated to generate an additional secondary impact roughly equal to one-third of the indirect effect of tourism.

An analysis of economic impacts in Tanzania indicates that induced effects are highly significant: their contribution to GDP is almost equivalent to all

Table 5.2 *Breakdown of secondary effects between indirect and induced effects in Singapore*

	Indirect	Induced	Ratio of indirect to induced impact
Income multiplier: Income impact of $1.00 tourist expenditure	$0.75	$0.23	3:1
Output multiplier: Output generated from every $1.00 tourist expenditure	$1.50	$0.50	3:1
Employment multiplier: number of jobs created per $1 million tourist expenditure	Direct and indirect: 27 jobs	6 jobs	4.5:1 (total direct plus indirect in relation to induced)

Source: Heng and Low, 1990

direct and indirect effects combined – and the scale of induced impacts is twice as large as indirect effects.

Scale of benefits to the poor from secondary linkages

Secondary effects are not just important because they involve large amounts of money – they can also involve large numbers of poor people. As researchers improve their understanding of the economies of tourist destinations, it is becoming clearer that much of the pro-poor impact of tourism occurs outside the tourism sector, and sometimes outside the immediate destination, through sometimes quite lengthy supply chains.

Recent value chain and economic mapping exercises have demonstrated empirically the importance of supply chains, particularly from agriculture, as a means for significant numbers of poor people to access meaningful benefits from the tourism sector. Results from a range of destinations are shown in Figure 5.1. In two of these, earnings from supply chains account for more than half of all the earnings of the poor from tourism.

Examining the composition of benefit flows to poor people, it is clear that indirect effects are often significant. In the contrasting destinations represented in Figure 5.1, about half the benefits to the poor from tourism are from indirect effects (the rest being mainly direct with a small number also including dynamic effects). The main sources of pro-poor benefit are food and craft supply to total tourism value. The importance of food supply varies with the availability of local produce and procurement patterns of the hotel and restaurant sector. The significance of craft as a conduit for pro-poor benefits varies mainly with the contrasting level of craft spending by tourists in the different destinations.

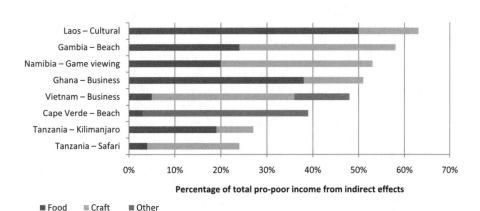

Source: Mitchell et al, 2009; Mitchell, 2008; Mitchell and Le Chi, 2007; Coles and Mitchell, 2009; Turpie et al, 2004; Mitchell and Faal, 2008; Ashley, 2006a

Figure 5.1 *Earnings of the poor from supply chains and inter-sectoral linkages*

There are other sources of indirect benefit transfers from tourists to poor people in tourist destinations. In the rapidly developing Cape Verdean tourism sector the wages paid to construction labourers are highly significant. In massage bars in Vietnamese business hotels the impact of sex workers is also an important pro-poor benefit flow.

Indirect effects are more muted in destinations where there are very significant direct pro-poor impacts (as with staff wages in Tanzania for both driver guides on safari and mountain climbing staff and park fees in both value chains, or hotel staff in Cape Verde).

Elsewhere, however, the findings from the macro-economic multiplier analysis above are corroborated with this destination-level pro-poor analysis. Indirect effects do not just involve large amounts of money; a significant share of these indirect financial flows also reach the poor.

In fact, it would appear there is some evidence from these data that indirect effects are disproportionately pro-poor compared with direct effects. The multiplier analysis suggested that indirect effects are generally 60–80 per cent as large financially as direct effects but, as a share of the benefits flowing to the poor, indirect effects are often more significant than direct effects. This suggests that, generally, indirect effects may be more pro-poor than direct effects.

It makes intuitive sense that the non-tourism sectors offer more opportunities for the poor. For instance, Lejárraga and Walkenhorst (2006, p19) state:

> With the exception of wages, most of the income generated through direct effects within the tourism economy goes to hotel and restaurant owners, namely local or international elites. By contrast, the income generated through indirect effects trickles down to the lower income layers of the economy. Since most of the industries that supply the tourism economy are non-high tech and labour intensive, the majority of backward linkages are forged by smaller unskilled producers. From a policy perspective, increasing the ratio multiplier promotes an equitable distribution of the tourism pie and offers a sustainable livelihood to smaller and lower-income producers in a broad array of economic sectors.

Assessments in The Gambia (Mitchell and Faal, 2007) and Laos (Ashley 2006a) provide examples where indirect impacts appear to be more pro-poor, at least compared to the narrowly defined accommodation and transport tourism sector. The share of accommodation revenue that reaches the poor is low (around 6–7 per cent), and accrues mainly through direct employment. The share of the food chain that reaches the poor is higher (around 20–45 per cent) accruing mainly through the supply of fresh food.

However, the reverse can also be true. An innovative CGE model analysis in Brazil concluded that the poor mainly benefit from the direct jobs in tourism – rather than the indirect impacts (Blake et al, 2008).

This analysis suggests that care should be taken making universal statements about the relative impacts on poor people of direct and indirect linkages. These are influenced by many geographically specific factors, like the quality and structure of local agriculture and tourist spending on craft, for instance. However, it is clear that indirect linkages can influence very large numbers of very poor people and add substantially to financial flows to the poor. The relative importance of both direct and indirect pathways, from tourism to the poor, should be assessed by policy makers at the destination level.

Benefits to the poor specifically from food supply chains

From a poverty perspective, the food supply chain into hotels and restaurants can be a particularly significant form of indirect benefit. This is because of its scale, and the variable but sometimes strong link between agriculture and the poor. In many developing country destinations, primary production of food is likely to involve poor people as smallholders or farm workers (even if the processing, marketing and other intermediaries are non-poor). As Telfer and Wall (1996) suggest, the degree to which the industry relies on imported food can significantly affect the social and economic impacts of tourism.

The potential development impact of the tourism food chain is evident in the literature. A number of sources indicate that food and beverages constitute about one-third of tourism expenditure and the great majority of this supply chain is serviced by domestic resources (SRI International, 1997; Torres, 2003). Economic assessment based on 1992 data in Tanzania estimates that half of the total employment impact of tourism is in the staple foods sector (Kweka et al, 2003). In Senegal, 35 per cent of local inputs used by tourism are agricultural and food products (Crompton and Christie, 2003). Referring to WTO (1998) data, Page (1999) reports that food expenditure is in the range of 18–20 per cent of total tourists' transactions.

Table 5.3 illustrates that food spending is almost as significant as local wage payments in two relatively well-developed destinations, Tunisia and the Dominican Republic. In both countries, the vast majority of food is sourced locally as the agricultural economy is well developed. Thus, if it can be assumed that roughly the same share of the food bill reaches the poor as the share of the wage bill, then this suggests that the indirect pathway of the food supply

Table 5.3 *The importance of food supply: Local food purchase compared to local wages*

Location	Hotel spend on domestic items, US$ million per annum		Food expenditure as % of wage expenditure
	Food	Wages	
Dominican Republic	72	78	93%
Tunisia	140	160	88%

Source: SRI International, 1997

chain is roughly as important as the direct pathway of formal employment for generating benefit flows to the poor.

This is an important 'if' because, as outlined in Chapter 4, there is reasonably robust evidence that in most destinations most hotel workers are from a poor background – so a reasonable share of the wages bill will accrue to the poor. This is more variable for the food supply chain.

While the literature clearly establishes the relative size of the food chain, there is less research on the extent to which the benefits reach the poor, or which farmers benefit by how much. What information does exist is more on whether food is procured from domestic sources rather than imported, on the implicit assumption that the former is more pro-poor than the latter. In some developing countries, particularly the Caribbean, researchers have questioned whether domestic agriculture has the supply capacity to serve the tourist market and highlighted the high level of agricultural imports needed to meet tourist demand (Meyer, 2006).

The evidence is very mixed and incomplete, but suggests that market failures, limited production and marketing capacity do limit access of poor producers to the tourism food chain. There are a number of supply, demand, and marketing constraints that can hamper procurement of food from local farmers (Torres, 2003; Telfer and Wall, 2000).

Nevertheless, studies that have collected information from hotels often find a surprising amount of food is procured locally. Even studies based upon the premise that agricultural linkages are inadequate, often find that the level of food imports is small and the challenge is to move agricultural production within the domestic economy closer to the immediate hinterland of the tourist destination (Torres and Momsen, 2005).

In Ethiopia, for instance, a very high proportion of food eaten by tourists is supplied from domestic sources (only 9 per cent of hotel food supplies in Addis are imported and none outside the capital). In addition to this, analysis of the supply chains (see Figure 5.2) revealed that they were dominated by large numbers of very small producers who were receiving a reasonably large share of the hotel input costs. Thus 44 per cent of total hotel expenditure on food was transmitted back to poor producers – an effective mechanism to transfer resources from tourists to the rural poor (Mitchell and Coles, 2009).

It is important to understand the pattern and the rationale for hotel and restaurant procurement practices. In central Vietnam, for instance, notwithstanding a reasonably strong local agricultural sector, the opening of a foreign-owned wholesaler offering competitive payment terms to the hospitality industry (and a global supply chain) had undermined the previously short local food supply chains. Some large resort chains will have an in-house supplier system and will not grant individual hotel managers the autonomy to purchase supplies locally – even if they are competitive.

The scope for policy and intervention to boost procurement of local food by hotels and restaurants and boost farmer earnings from food supply is widely regarded as considerable (Wagner, 1997; Telfer and Wall, 2000; Lengefeld and Stewart, 2004; Ashley and Mitchell, 2006). There is some robust evidence

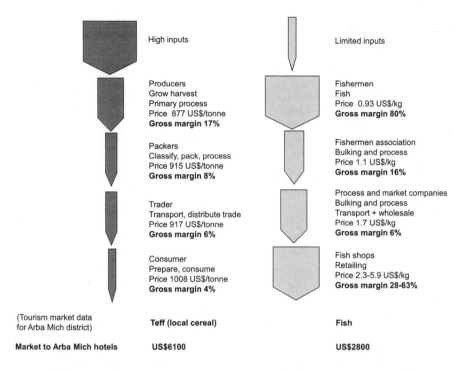

High inputs

Producers
Grow harvest
Primary process
Price 877 US$/tonne
Gross margin 17%

Packers
Classify, pack, process
Price 915 US$/tonne
Gross margin 8%

Trader
Transport, distribute trade
Price 917 US$/tonne
Gross margin 6%

Consumer
Prepare, consume
Price 1008 US$/tonne
Gross margin 4%

Limited inputs

Fishermen
Fish
Price 0.93 US$/kg
Gross margin 80%

Fishermen association
Bulking and process
Price 1.1 US$/kg
Gross margin 16%

Process and market companies
Bulking and process
Transport + wholesale
Price 1.7 US$/kg
Gross margin 6%

Fish shops
Retailing
Price 2.3-5.9 US$/kg
Gross margin 28-63%

(Tourism market data
for Arba Mich district)

Market to Arba Mich hotels

Teff (local cereal)

US$6100

Fish

US$2800

Source: Adapted from Mitchell and Coles, 2009

Figure 5.2 *Fish and teff food supply chains in Ethiopia compared*

that initiatives of this kind have delivered positive outcomes (see the oft-cited Sandals example in Box 5.4). However, generally the results of agricultural linkage programmes have been disappointing. Successful initiatives often need to work on the supply side (to increase the quantity, quality and consistency of suppliers), the demand side (to ensure a market for the produce), with intermediaries (to provide working capital to reconcile the disjuncture between hotel payment terms and cash-flow requirements of farmers) and the enabling environment for linkages.

To date, studies of tourist destinations indicate the importance of local food supply links where these are well established. However, the experience of initiatives to improve local linkages has not been very encouraging and is generally much more difficult than most development practitioners assume.

Generally, initiatives to enhance indirect linkages have been much more effective in the craft and construction sector than in the agricultural sector.

Which poor people benefit?

Indirect linkages affect three main groups of poor people. The first is farmers and intermediaries who sell the food destined for hotels and restaurants.

Box 5.4 *Impact on farmers of boosting access to the tourism food supply chain in the Caribbean*

A clear example of how farmers benefit from improved food sales to hotels comes from Jamaica (Lengefeld and Stewart, 2004). The Sandals Resort Farmers Programme, initiated and supported by the Sandals Group, began in 1996 with ten farmers supplying two hotels. By 2004, there were 80 farmers supplying hotels across the island. Impacts for farmers are clear. Purchases of watermelon and cantaloupe by just one Sandals resort of $7200 per month translates into a monthly income of $100 for 70 families, taking them above the poverty line. As a result of the overall programme, farmers' sales increased over 55 times in 3 years, from $60,000 to $3.3 million.

An example of the potential development significance to agriculture of a shift in tourism food procurement is given by the Agro-Tourism Linkages Centre of the Inter-American Institute for Cooperation on Agriculture (IICA, Barbados) which states:

> After 'Accommodation', 'Food and Beverage' represents the second highest area of expenditure in the tourism sector. With a reported leakage of 60 to 80 cents of every tourism dollar spent in some Caribbean countries, some analysts estimate that an effective linkage between agriculture and tourism would dramatically reduce the Caribbean's import bill by hundreds of millions of dollars, while giving agriculture a greater economic stake at a time when the banana and sugar industries seem to be on their last legs (cited in Ashley and Mitchell, 2006, p1).

Depending upon the quality of rural infrastructure and agricultural potentials, producers may be anywhere in the country, or indeed other countries, and are certainly not confined to the destination. This should not be regarded as a bad thing because it implies that the developmental benefits of tourist spending are not confined to the vicinity of tourist destinations but rather spread deep into the least advantaged rural areas. This can allow farmers who may never meet a tourist to still benefit from the trade in tourism services.

The second group is a diverse range of micro and informal entrepreneurs who provide local goods and services such as laundry, security, construction and consumable goods to the tourism sector. These supply chains will tend to be short – so beneficiaries will almost all be located within the tourist destination itself.

The third group are the unskilled workers in non-tourism sectors that supply inputs, such as in construction, craft, furnishing and light manufacture. These beneficiaries may be located anywhere within (or outside) the host country.

We have only recently started looking at the pro-poor impact of tourist facility construction and have been struck by the divergent impact in different destinations. In some destinations, hotel construction is highly pro-poor. For instance, in destinations on the Northern Historical Route and Southern Cultural Route in Ethiopia, relatively modest hotels are having a significant positive impact on the local economy and poor people within it. Large numbers of construction workers from predominantly poor backgrounds are engaged in extremely labour-intensive construction techniques using materials with high local content. The impact of this is that between one-quarter and one-third of capital investment costs are benefiting the local poor.

Contrast this with the situation in Addis Ababa where system-build construction techniques are being applied by a much more highly skilled workforce to materials that are 90 per cent imported (and benefiting from duty-free import incentives). In the capital only about 4 per cent of capital investment costs are benefiting the local poor (Mitchell and Coles, 2009).

Factors affecting scale and distribution of indirect flows to the poor

It is self-evident that if a hotel or restaurant imports its tomatoes and bananas, then they are not sourced domestically and potential indirect impacts may be displaced by imports – so propensity to import matters. It is also fairly clear that there are some critical factors that determine the share of tourism supplies that are sourced domestically, such as the level of development of the host economy: a larger more diversified economy can supply more of the needs of its tourism industry itself.

However, beyond these obvious points, there lies a host of assertions, assumptions, confusions and a few policy-relevant points about imports, linkages and so-called leakages. This section summarizes a few of the findings on factors that influence procurement via imports versus domestic supply chains. However, one problem in analysing the literature is that it is not always clear when authors' figures for import 'leakage' are actually using a wider, and we consider erroneous, leakage concept as discussed below.

There is some consensus on some key factors that affect the balance of domestic sourcing versus imports:

- *Larger and more developed economies support lower linkages* (Smith and Jenner, 1992; Lejárraga and Walkenhorst, 2006). A report produced by the Economic Commission for Africa suggests that developing countries with diversified economies have leakages of 10–20 per cent, and 40–50 per cent in smaller economies, with leakage figures peaking at 75 per cent in The Gambia (Gerosa, 2003).
- *A certain scale of tourism is required to stimulate other sectors of the economy* (Smith and Jenner, 1992). Tourism needs to reach sufficient scale for linkages to become viable. Conversely, the geographical dispersion

of tourism can reduce linkages by reducing the potential advantages of economies of scale and critical mass for suppliers.

- *Linkages vary over time.* The notion that domestic supply firms develop through time along with tourism is well established in the literature, and discussed further in Chapter 6. There may be a twin peak in leakages from the pioneering stage when tourism would be low. As tourism expands, imports are sucked in. As the non-tourism economy expands, a greater proportion of needs can again be met locally until finally leakages rise again as the share of trade in GDP expands relative to agriculture (Smith and Jenner, 1992).
- *The business environment* and functioning of the market affects the capacity of small firms to respond to needs of the tourism sector and the capacity of tourism firms to tap into local business networks. Efficiency of communication, transport, pricing and market services are all relevant.
- *Different types of tourism* have different spending patterns and requirements (Smith and Jenner, 1992; Archer and Fletcher, 1996). In a small economy, tourist experiences that are dependent on safari jeeps, bottled water and expatriate staff are likely to have a different balance of local and imported components than back-packers, budget and domestic tourists.

Some of these are 'given' in the short- to medium-term, such as the size and degree of diversification of the host economy and the size of tourism. But this does not imply that there is little that policy can do to enhance linkages, particularly on the supply side. The recent literature emphasizes the importance of the entrepreneurial and institutional environment. As Kweka et al (2003) pointed out in highlighting the estimated indirect impact of tourism (from static input–output model analysis) in Tanzania: 'expanding the sector offers a potential stimulus to the entire economy, but other sectors need to be enabled to respond to that stimulus' (p348). The failure of linkages to improve over the past 20 years prompts the researchers to suggest there has been a lack of sustained and integrated government support for this outcome.

A regression analysis of linkage and import leakage data for 151 countries suggested that inherent or given factors have a relatively small influence on the degree of inter-sectoral linkage, and that the key influential factors are within the domain of policy makers. Lejárraga and Walkenhorst (2006, p28), found that the most influential variables affecting linkages are as follows:

- Natural endowments: capital and agricultural machinery (but not land or labour).
- Socio-economic development: human development index, Gini coefficient and gender participation.
- Institutions: degree of democracy, informal sector activity, crime and violence.
- Business environment: business start-up costs, corporate tax rate, labour market regulation and internet usage.

- Trade policy: most favoured nation tariffs, non-tariff barriers, degree of diversification and signatures required for imports.

The key policy implications from this analysis are first that there is not one single area of action for policy makers to address, but many. Boosting linkages involves a multi-faceted approach. Second, that several of these variables are amenable to short- or medium-term policy influence, and in fact the variables that are most amenable – trade and business environment – have a disproportionately large impact on the development of linkages. Third, leakages are determined by a somewhat different set of factors, being more influenced by inherent natural endowments, plus world factors that are external to the country. Thus adopting policies to promote linkages is different to, and more likely to be effective than, reducing leakages.

The business environment is found to explain over half of the variation between countries in the extent of inter-sectoral linkages with tourism according to the analysis. This is important because the annual competitiveness league tables for travel and tourism produced by the World Economic Forum (WEF) underline the poor performance of African governments in maintaining a conducive regulatory environment for tourism development (WEF, 2007). The business environment particularly is also seen as a key factor in the degree of linkage with informal business.

Why 'leakage' is not a helpful concept

The term 'leakage' is used in several contrasting ways by different types of tourism researcher. Confusion between the definitions used by economists for calculating net receipts and income multipliers and the definitions used by practitioners and campaigners for criticizing tourism is just one of the reasons why research on leakage is of little help in understanding factors that enhance linkages.

Share of tourist receipts that accrues overseas The most straightforward concept of leakage is that it represents the share of receipts from incoming foreigners that accrue overseas. It thus represents the import coefficient of tourism. As Smith and Jenner put it in 1992:

> *The real economic benefit of tourism to any country or community is not revealed by gross foreign exchange earnings but by the proportion retained after deducting the foreign exchange costs of tourism. Purchases of imported equipment, foodstuffs, fuel and so on – often vital inputs for tourism – obviously reduce the amount of earnings retained within the destination economy* (Smith and Jenner, 1992, p1).

In addition to imports of capital goods or consumables, this type of leakage also included charges on foreign debt incurred for tourism development, overseas tourism promotion by nationals, employment of foreigners, repatriation of profits by foreign companies and depreciation of infrastructure.

The important thing to note here is that leakage is a proportion of a country's international tourism receipts (a technical term measuring foreign currency earnings from foreign tourists). That is, it is based on funds that accrue in the destination country, not on the total spending of tourists who arrive. In this sense, leakages are the opposite of inter-sectoral linkages, and indicate areas where domestic linkages might be enhanced.

As Smith and Jenner (1992) pointed out, leakages reduce the net foreign exchange benefits from tourism, but action to reduce leakages (such as taxes) can also reduce total earnings from tourism so must be handled with care.

The share of direct and indirect tourism activity that accrues overseas This is a more nuanced version of the first definition of leakage, which takes into account that the non-tourism sectors that supply tourism, and the staff who earn wages from tourism, can also generate leakages. It would be an over-simplification to calculate the economic benefits of tourism by assuming that 100 per cent of the indirect and induced impacts stay within the domestic economy. The leakage figure for tourism should therefore take into account the import coefficient of the tourism industry, the supply chain and the workers.

Using this definition, tourism can generate high inter-sectoral linkages as well as high import leakages. The sector may draw in many domestically produced inputs, such as in food, construction, manufacturing and energy, meaning that a unit of direct tourism output generates another unit of indirect output in the other sectors. But at the same time, leakage can be high because those supplying sectors rely on imports (Lejárraga and Walkenhorst, 2006). Malaysia is an example of this apparent paradox. Tourism there stimulates considerable activity in other sectors of the economy, and the non-tourism economy has a high propensity to import. The net effect of this is a tourism sector with both high linkages and high leakages (Cernat and Gourdon, 2005).

The co-existence of high leakages and inter-sectoral linkages has further policy implications. Strengthening inter-sectoral linkages from tourism does not necessarily mean reducing the overall leakage rate. Conversely, actions to prevent leakages arising from overall tourism activity may actually hinder the indirect linkages between tourism and non-tourism sectors.

The share of tourist spending that does not reach, or does not remain in the destination Over the last decade, negative claims about tourism's limited development contribution have often been based on claims about high 'leakage' rates. However, on closer inspection they appear to be using a quite different definition of leakage, because they are based on the holiday purchase price (or package price) paid by the tourist from his/her home.

These approaches (examples in Box 5.5) include in 'leakage' those payments for booking, insurance and travel services that are provided by companies overseas and not in the destination. Smith and Jenner (1992) referred to these elements of travel price that never reach the destination as 'pre-leakage'. To

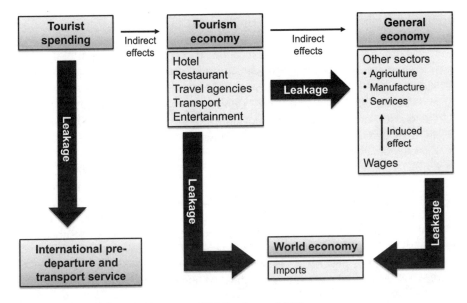

Source: Adapted from Lejárraga and Walkenhorst, 2006

Figure 5.3 *Illustration of linkages, leakages and pre-leakages*

include these items in leakage statistics is tantamount to regarding the revenue of a coffee stand at Heathrow as a leakage from the Ethiopian coffee farmers who supply the coffee. There are other problems too with this approach. The data based on holiday cost tend to use the package holiday price, and thus ignore precisely the component of tourism expenditure that has high poverty impact – out-of-pocket spending. Because of a lack of good empirical data the claims tend to be based on very old recycled data, which get further distorted over time.

Another problem with this approach, important from a policy point of view, is that by hyping up concern over marketing and booking margins at the top of the tourism chain, and creating the sense that these leakages are the opposite of desired local linkage, they divert policy attention away from the practical question of how to boost local linkages within a destination.

So what is the significance of this discussion of 'leakages' in the literature for our findings on the poverty impacts of tourism? First, it is another example of how loose and conflicting terms lead to claims that are not useful for policy but instead obfuscate important development choices.

Second, the share of the holiday cost that reaches the destination is, of course, one matter for attention. If a destination can gain more of the pre-departure price paid by the tourist, for example, by shifting from heavy marketing structures to web marketing, then this would increase the total tourism pie in the destination. Possible trade-offs need to be explored of course, such as effects on volumes of arrivals, or subsidy costs of an airline that on the surface appears to 'capture' a higher share of tourism revenue for the country.

Box 5.5 *Examples of misuse and misinterpretation of 'leakage'*

It is often claimed that about 80 per cent of tourism income leaks out of the economy in Kenya. The claim can be sourced to a gloomy reading of Hemmati and Koehler (2000, p27) that states, 'Concerning 14-night beach-only holidays, the total foreign exchange leakage going back to the overseas tour operator and airline ranged between 62 per cent and 78 per cent'. These figures are, in turn, sourced from analysis by Sinclair (1991).

There are several problems in using the original data to support an 80 per cent leakage claim. For one thing, the analysis was in the days when the airfare accounted for 50 per cent of the beach holiday price. Thus for tourists not flying Kenya Air, the share staying in Kenya could only ever be a fraction of 50 per cent. For another, 80 per cent is the most pessimistic figure: according to Sinclair's figures, 78 per cent was the highest percentage that would accrue outside Kenya. Lower rates of 62 per cent, 45 per cent, 34 per cent 18 per cent and 12 per cent were calculated for other months, for other types of package (that include safari), and if Kenya Airways is used.

The greatest problem, however, is in using these figures to define 'leakage'. Firstly, the denominator is inappropriate: the original Sinclair article makes clear that the analysis was only of expenditure in the UK by tourists on inclusive tour packages. It excludes in-country out-of-pocket spending, which would be essential for assessing flows within the local economy. The denominator should be either all holiday spending or, preferably, all spending for goods and services provided within the destination. The numerator – the amount of package price that accrues in the UK – also seems misconceived. Funds that are paid in the UK for UK services do not represent a 'leakage' out of Kenya anymore than Starbucks revenue that goes towards costs of running a high street café represent a 'leakage' to coffee producing countries. It is difficult to see how this 80 per cent 'leakage' is of any use to policymaking in Kenya in 2007.

Sinclair (1998) pointed out in 1998 that calculation of the multiplier is quite different to the issue of the share of the holiday package that accrues domestically (what some people call leakage). The multiplier measures the ratio between an initial increase in final demand in tourism within the economy, and the eventual total increase in demand once demand in other sectors, and loss of demand to imports, are taken into account. The initial increase, therefore, comes from expenditure that reaches the destination. A separate point is to ask how much of the holiday cost reaches the destination in the first place, and whether the destination can capture a greater share of revenue relating to marketing and packaging the product. Thus she explained that a country could be receiving a small absolute amount from tourism because of revenues accruing to tour operators and others higher in the chain, but still appear to have high multipliers because of linkages with other sectors.

However, reducing the share of tourist spend that is captured by overseas service providers is a different issue to how to make best development use of tourists' spending power once they are in the country. Policy issues here are about boosting their discretionary spending, and stimulating linkages from core tourism to other parts of the economy. A reduction in imports may be a result of successful linkage creation, but that is a different policy objective and strategy to one that aims to reduce pre-leakage.

Factors affecting flows to the poor from indirect linkages

There is a strong emphasis in the PPT literature on strategies that enhance linkages that are local and involve small enterprises. The implicit assumption here is that small and local suppliers are more likely to be poor.[1]

The overall business environment for small enterprises is important. It is no surprise that in entrepreneurial economies such as Laos and Vietnam, small and micro enterprises are clearly active in the supply chain (Ashley, 2006a; Mitchell and Le Chi, 2007). In contrast, examples of market failure are evident in South Africa where apartheid created durable barriers between potential users and providers of services. The Highlands Meander (Rogerson, 2002) is an example of a tourism route that has expanded successfully, but with notably few linkages developing with small enterprises owned by formerly disadvantaged black entrepreneurs. Also in South Africa, Relly (2004a) points out that in Madikwe Game Reserve, targeted support to small, medium and micro enterprises (SMMEs) meant that some local suppliers were able to develop as the park developed and as economies of scale became possible. However, in this context, where linkages do not occur naturally, there is a considerable emphasis on the need for intervention and SMME support to stimulate them, and meanwhile employment remains the dominant source of local income.

Even where government has progressive policies, ensuring their implementation can be problematic. A case study in northeast Brazil has found that most stakeholders agree that an important objective of tourism development should be to benefit the poor and this goal has been written into planning documents. The concern is that these pro-poor policies, such as economic linkage programmes, were simply not implemented (Siegel and Alwang, 2005).

Case studies also illustrate the difference that corporate action can make. Again in South Africa, a few enterprises stand out for having high or increasing local sourcing due to a commitment by the hotel. Umngazi River Bungalows (Eastern Cape) takes pride in the fact that 70 per cent of its fresh fruit and vegetables, plus considerable supplies of fresh fish, come from local farmers, and invested heavily in creating linkages at the start (Kirsten and Rogerson, 2002). Spier Village (Western Cape) is increasing its procurement from local black businesses through strategic overhaul of its supply chain and procurement. It estimates that if it achieves its target of shifting 10 per cent of corporate procurement, then this would deliver a greater boost to local income than a 50 per cent boost in local staff wages (Ashley and Haysom, 2006).

Table 5.4 *Strengthening the type of linkages between tourism and agriculture*

Demand related factors	Supply related factors	Marketing and intermediary factors	Government policy
The type of visitor accommodation: ownership, size and quality	Physical limitations	Marketing and infrastructure constraints	Extent of planning, resourcing and providing quality advice and inputs
Tourism industry maturity	Entrenched production patterns (e.g. plantation crops for export)	Supply poorly adjusted to demand	
Promotion of local cuisine	Quantity and quality of local production	Spatial patterns of supply	
Health and safety concerns	High prices of locally produced food	Agreements/contract/ kickbacks	
Training and nationality of chefs	Technological and processing limitations	Industry standards	
Seasonality	Competition for labour	Distribution infrastructure	
	Undercapitalization of the agrarian sector	Middle men	

Source: Adapted from Meyer, 2006

More detailed analysis of factors that impede or support local sourcing has been done specifically on agricultural supply chains, again on the implicit assumption that these chains reach the poor. A summary of literature from Meyer (2006) presents factors related to demand (from chefs, hotels, tourists), supply (the nature of the agricultural economy), the functioning of the market between farmer and tourism, and government policy. It should be noted that some of these are referring to domestic (national) sourcing of food, while others are referring to sourcing from the locality.

There is a growing literature on the role of policy, project interventions and corporate behaviour in strengthening local food supply chains. An analysis of failed interventions in Cancun (Torres, 2003) illustrates what is also evident from Table 5.4. An effective programme of linkage must be multi-faceted: it has to address issues relating to demand, supply, the interface between the two, and supportive government policy.

The micro examples available suggest that the role of chefs and of corporate commitment can make a difference to local linkages (Torres, 2003; Lengefeld and Stewart, 2004; Piccini, 1999). In the example from the Sandals programme in Jamaica, referred to above, a key success factor was bringing together the resort and local farmers (Lengefeld and Stewart, 2004). The programme involved agricultural extension and a variety of methods of

Box 5.6 *Examples of supply-side constraints in agricultural supply*

Weak supply-side capacity can prevent hotels and restaurants buying local products:

> Most of the fresh produce needed by the tourism industry is imported from producers in nearby Trinidad and from importers based there. Business links with Tobago suppliers were limited to fresh fish, lobsters and farm eggs. The absence of six critical success factors – competitive price, consistent quality, wide variety, reliability of supply, access to credit facilities and business acumen – were found to be responsible for the poor performance of the local supply chain, giving Trinidad suppliers the competitive advantage over Tobago businesses (Abdool and Carey, 2004, pi).

Other examples include the fact that 4 and 5 star hotels in Rwanda (a tea producer) use imported tea, since Rwandan tea is not supplied in individually wrapped bags (Verdugo, 2007). In Mozambique, domestic supply is limited by the highly competitive bulk supply available from South Africa (Sarmento, 2007).

strengthening communication and market information between hotels and farmers. In other cases, challenges have arisen in issues of political economy and reluctance on the part of developing country urban elites to interact with and trust poor, rural communities (Torres, 2003).

In summary, the evidence on benefits to the poor via indirect impacts of tourism is piecemeal, but does indicate that this is a highly significant route for poverty impact in many destinations. There are little data on which poor benefit and by how much from supplying goods and services to the tourism sector. There is, nevertheless, relatively clear evidence of the main factors that determine how much of the supply chain is procured domestically, and particularly from local small suppliers. While some of these are relatively fixed over the medium to long term, such as the supply capacity of the destination economy and the scale of tourism, there are also several variables amenable to policy influence. Areas for intervention are on the supply side – such as the business environment and support for small and micro enterprise; demand side – such as attitudes of chefs and hotels; and in the functioning of the market that enables suppliers and purchasers to engage more efficiently in transactions.

Notes

1   This assumption has not been tested. Intuitively, where procurement is directly with local small businesses and does not involve large wholesalers

or corporate and long-distance transport, it would be expected that the share staying with relatively low income people would be greater. But that said, it is conceptually feasible for bulk wholesale purchases of food, furnishings and construction material to generate as much or more in income to unskilled labour as local MSE purchasing.

6
Pathway 3: Dynamic Effects on Macro and Local Economies

The tourism sector may also stimulate longer-term dynamic effects, in addition to the direct and indirect static effects that occur in the same period as tourism spending. The theory on dynamic effects is not strong and many economists working with neo-classical models are unable to account for how structural change occurs in the economy. There is virtually no assessment of how dynamic effects specifically impact the poor (with the exception of transport investment). However, dynamic effects are potentially large and should not be ignored. It is possible that most of the poverty-alleviating effects from tourism development in the long run are derived from the dynamic effects of pathway 3.

In this brief review we identify a number of channels through which the tourism sector may affect the rest of the economy in the longer term:

- infrastructure, public and social goods;
- human resource development (e.g. training of workforce);
- private sector development (especially small and medium enterprise (SME) development and entrepreneurship);
- changes to the production structure of the economy;
- trajectories of long-term development;
- linkages between sectors.

These effects can operate at various levels, ranging from local to national. A number may be felt particularly at the destination level and thus in combination may be seen as drivers of local economic development. A range of studies that have considered the effects of tourism on the national economy are relevant for this chapter, even though they may not have explored the transmission mechanism explicitly. Finally, there is evidence to suggest that the strength of the various effects depends on complementary policies (infrastructure and human resource development itself), institutions and economic conditions.

Infrastructure, and public and social goods

Tourism growth is an important source of incentives and resources to strengthen the infrastructure network at local, regional or national level. On the demand side, tourism activity needs infrastructure, such as efficient transportation, communications and distribution networks, in order to flourish. This may act as an incentive for government to improve public goods, which may be important for increasing the productivity of the tourism sector but also the rest of the economy. Torres (2003), in her analysis of the missed opportunity for high value agricultural produce in the agricultural hinterland of the Cancun in Mexico (Quintana Roo Region), provides a reminder that infrastructure is not only a hardware issue. The opportunity was that tourist infrastructure resulted in an airport and flights with competitive freight rates to major markets in the US and the European Union. However, additional infrastructure will not always lead to economic development elsewhere; because of a lack of government programmes to support local agricultural producers, poor farmers were not able to respond positively to this enhanced infrastructure.

Subramanian and Matthijs (2007) point to another example of a dynamic effect of tourism in Kenya. Increased flights required for tourism reduced the cost of airfreight to Europe and provided new transport opportunities for small quantities of fresh products. Tourism also increased local demand for high quality fruit and vegetables and provided a market for produce that did not meet export standards. More generally, they argue that by positioning itself as a relatively close and attractive holiday destination, the gain for sub-Saharan Africa is not just felt within the tourism sector. More frequent direct flights arriving in African airports make transport cheaper and export markets more readily accessible for African goods.

On the supply side, the growth in tourism should lead to more tax revenues through income, sales and corporation taxes, which, in turn, can help towards the provision of public and social goods, such as infrastructure. Much depends on the tax intake of the larger hotels. The tourism sector is among the largest foreign exchange earners in several of the least developed countries with the most intractable poverty problems.

Improved infrastructure can help spread benefits from the tourism sector's growth specifically to the rural poor. Kweka (2004) provides an account of how a programme of rural infrastructure that reduces transport costs can impact on the distributional effects of tourism growth in Tanzania. Without improved rural infrastructure, welfare gains of a 10 per cent increase in international tourist expenditure are concentrated in urban areas. Rural households actually suffer a decline in welfare as their main source of livelihood incomes, agricultural exports, lose competitiveness on international markets as tourist receipts lead to an appreciation of the exchange rate. However, this loss of competitiveness can be more than offset with an infrastructure programme that improves the accessibility of – and reduces costs to – Tanzania's rural hinterland. This policy intervention allows rural households to make welfare gains twice the level of urban households.

Human resource development

The tourism sector can enhance human resource development. It strengthens incentives for households to invest in training. It also furthers development of its workforce though formal and informal on-the-job training at the workplace. As the development of the tourist industry crucially depends on the availability of appropriate skills in the country, human resource development is important for tourist industry growth. This may provide a strong incentive for the sector to develop those skills needed which are not available, by investing in training and education. This is critical in terms of broadening the beneficiaries from PPT to include active participation from the poor (see Scheyvens, 2007). As with all forms of human capital accumulation, such investments are likely to have positive spillover effects onto the rest of the economy.

Meyer (2006) argues that there are a wide variety of case studies on the involvement and contribution of tourism enterprises to 'training up' the local work force and to providing general educational and SME support. She classifies the role that a tourism enterprise can play in providing training, education and capacity building into four categories:

1 in-house training;
2 build up of new capacity: tourism-related education in secondary, tertiary and higher education;
3 general education: support to schools (e.g. donations, lectures and courses, course material, internships, scholarships); tourism awareness raising among the population;
4 supplier support (e.g. business training along backwards linkages).

Apart from training its own workforce, the main ways in which businesses have in the past supported education was through the third category. In recent years, however, businesses have also increasingly become involved in tertiary and higher education by actively supporting, designing and financing technical and degree courses in tourism management. Evidence of the impact of 'mentoring' small suppliers is anecdotal but very positive, as seen in examples of Calabash Tours, Jan Harmsgat Country House and Spier Village hotel in South Africa, where experienced white tourism operators assist small entrepreneurs to develop their own capacity (Ashley et al, 2005).

Within the hotel chains there is some evidence of an increasing investment in staff training, though both employers and workers often fail to understand its importance. Employers may employ and promote staff on the basis of personality rather than formal qualifications, although at management level post-secondary education is generally required (ILO, 2001).

Changes to the structure of the economy

The tourism sector may also alter the production structure of the economy. Because of its large international trade component and large weight in several

Table 6.1 *Findings of WEF Travel and Tourism Competitiveness Index, 2007*

Country/Economy	Regulatory framework		Policy rules and regulations		Environmental regulation		Safety and security		Health and hygiene		Prioritization of travel and tourism	
	Rank	Score	Rank	Score	Rank	Score	Rank	Score	Rank	Score	Rank	Score
Algeria	89	3.81	113	3.37	82	3.66	74	4.18	53	4.91	109	2.92
Angola	122	2.91	121	2.93	115	2.92	92	3.85	119	2.61	121	2.27
Bangladesh	121	3.07	99	3.69	112	2.96	119	3.08	105	3.27	118	2.37
Benin	112	3.40	119	3.22	76	3.75	82	4.09	113	3.12	110	2.84
Botswana	64	4.21	59	4.74	59	4.11	55	4.65	86	4.09	83	3.45
Burkina Faso	102	3.58	105	3.65	57	4.16	65	4.47	120	2.59	103	3.05
Burundi	123	2.82	122	2.92	118	2.85	108	3.45	111	3.16	124	1.75
Cambodia	90	3.77	93	3.78	73	3.82	98	3.72	122	2.21	7	5.34
Cameroon	119	3.16	111	3.39	116	2.91	89	4.01	110	3.19	119	2.32
Chad	124	2.51	123	2.78	123	2.62	120	2.98	123	1.78	117	2.38
China	78	4.00	97	3.76	88	3.53	83	4.08	84	4.09	33	4.54
Egypt	50	4.52	69	4.59	75	3.79	64	4.54	69	4.50	12	5.18
Ethiopia	120	3.13	115	3.33	111	2.98	58	4.60	124	1.67	102	3.10
Gambia, The	52	4.48	74	4.38	43	4.41	48	4.80	95	3.81	20	4.98
Hong Kong SAR	4	5.75	2	5.76	24	5.11	6	6.07	1	6.62	13	5.18
India	62	4.24	86	4.12	41	4.45	39	4.96	100	3.59	48	4.06
Indonesia	54	4.45	43	4.97	81	3.66	50	4.77	103	3.48	6	5.36
Japan	28	5.10	38	5.05	17	5.47	23	5.37	28	5.78	63	3.85
Kenya	91	3.76	116	3.33	60	4.07	116	3.12	106	3.26	19	4.99
Korea, Rep.	46	4.61	56	4.78	37	4.60	37	5.00	60	4.78	58	3.87
Lesotho	116	3.34	87	4.04	105	3.17	94	3.80	109	3.21	115	2.46
Madagascar	104	3.54	117	3.23	62	3.98	93	3.81	118	2.69	50	3.99
Malawi	103	3.57	73	4.45	86	3.56	81	4.09	104	3.28	114	2.47

Country/Economy	Regulatory framework		Policy rules and regulations		Environmental regulation		Safety and security		Health and hygiene		Prioritization of travel and tourism	
	Rank	Score	Rank	Score	Rank	Score	Rank	Score	Rank	Score	Rank	Score
Malaysia	27	5.12	26	5.25	20	5.31	26	5.30	62	4.75	21	4.98
Mali	93	3.72	110	3.45	69	3.87	66	4.45	114	3.12	66	3.71
Mauritania	95	3.68	112	3.38	98	3.34	54	4.71	115	3.05	55	3.90
Mongolia	92	3.74	94	3.78	117	2.87	77	4.13	75	4.26	68	3.66
Morocco	47	4.60	48	4.90	64	3.97	43	4.88	81	4.11	15	5.16
Mozambique	115	3.34	108	3.50	91	3.48	100	3.60	121	2.50	72	3.64
Namibia	73	4.05	44	4.95	48	4.32	85	4.07	107	3.23	69	3.66
Nepal	113	3.39	91	3.83	97	3.35	123	2.73	116	3.02	49	4.04
Nigeria	118	3.32	109	3.49	78	3.69	117	3.10	108	3.21	101	3.10
Pakistan	106	3.50	98	3.73	85	3.57	106	3.46	91	4.04	111	2.71
Philippines	80	3.98	61	4.72	83	3.65	96	3.75	77	4.22	74	3.59
Singapore	1	5.81	1	5.78	6	5.92	7	6.02	29	5.77	2	5.57
South Africa	59	4.35	46	4.94	28	4.97	95	3.77	82	4.10	51	3.99
Sri Lanka	70	4.11	64	4.67	74	3.80	112	3.27	70	4.49	37	4.33
Tanzania	72	4.07	101	3.68	44	4.40	79	4.09	101	3.55	31	4.61
Thailand	41	4.78	55	4.78	39	4.58	42	4.91	59	4.80	25	4.84
Tunisia	12	5.34	42	4.98	16	5.47	14	5.64	52	5.02	1	5.59
Uganda	105	3.54	103	3.66	66	3.94	109	3.44	112	3.13	79	3.51
Vietnam	84	3.91	104	3.66	84	3.59	51	4.77	94	3.96	76	3.55
Zambia	86	3.87	58	4.76	95	3.39	70	4.33	117	2.69	43	4.15
Zimbabwe	108	3.49	114	3.36	90	3.51	86	4.07	102	3.48	105	3.04

Source: WEF, 2007

Note: Rank is the rating of each country out of the 124 nations evaluated (with descending order of performance) and the score out of 10 awarded

developing economies, the effects of tourism on the incentives for the allocation of resources across sectors may be significant, and hence will affect the structure of factor and product markets.

A further dynamic effect of tourism is the encouragement of entrepreneurship and development of firms, in particular among smaller firms. This is because some tourist activities, such as tourist guides, tourist agencies and transport operations, do not require large investments, and may be fairly profitable. Ennew (2003) cites empirical research suggesting that special interest tourism may be particularly conducive to the development of entrepreneurship. Having gained some experience, skills can then be applied elsewhere in the labour market. This is confirmed by micro livelihoods analysis, with examples of individuals who benefit in this way (Murphy and Halstead, 2003).

In Bali, craft and small scale tourism are a more appropriate means of achieving development objectives than large mainstream tourism, and these lesser scales of enterprise match the general scale of the Balinese economy and society (Rodenburg, 1980). On the other hand, Jenkins (1982), in his critique, indicates that large scale developments are likely to be inevitable, due to the external economies of scale and market structures in international tourism, but that the consequences of these developments can be mitigated by appropriate pre-project planning.

Williams (1998) developed a model for illustrating the development of tourism entrepreneurship and linkages in a developing world context (see Figure 6.1). This is captured in a simplified form in a three-stage model of entrepreneurial development, based on experience in the Caribbean. Burgess and Venables (2004, p19) explain how when growth (in any sector) reaches a sufficient size, it can create thicker factor markets, thus creating further advantages for growth: 'thick market effects arise when increased volumes of trade in a particular market increase the efficiency with which the market operates. A number of mechanisms give rise to such effects, including improved matching of buyers and sellers, reduced monopoly or monopsony power, and the development of specialist suppliers – a finer division of labour'. While the Williams model is standard in tourism texts, there does not appear to have been any assessment of this dynamic effect in the tourism sector.

Although governments have considerable experience in supporting small businesses to access viable supply chains, in practice their record has demonstrated an inability to provide the kind of consistent and targeted support that allows a sustainable market to develop in local economies in the hinterland of tourist resorts. As work by the Small Business Project has shown, such constraints can have a disproportionate affect on SMEs. Furthermore, analysis in South Africa reinforces the message that tourism suffers particularly from a poor business environment. Small Business Project research shows that the average annual recurring compliance costs per firm in the tourism sector may be up to three times higher than for other firms in the broader economy (SBP, 2005).

On the negative side there is an embryonic literature in tourism studies examining the potential for tourist booms as a demand phenomenon to

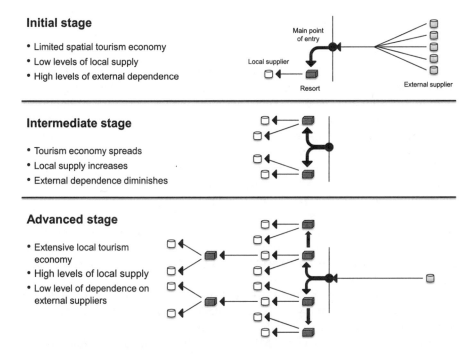

Initial stage

- Limited spatial tourism economy
- Low levels of local supply
- High levels of external dependence

Intermediate stage

- Tourism economy spreads
- Local supply increases
- External dependence diminishes

Advanced stage

- Extensive local tourism economy
- High levels of local supply
- Low level of dependence on external suppliers

Source: Adapted from Williams, 1998

Figure 6.1 *A model of business linkages and tourism*

negatively impact the rest of the economy in the same way as has been noted for supply oriented 'shocks' – like the discovery of oil (Nowak and Sahli, 2007). The concept is straightforward. Inbound tourist booms result in a surge of foreign currency that can cause the appreciation of the external value of the domestic currency – that can make exports less competitive. A tourist boom can also increase domestic prices. Both these effects (appreciating currency and domestic inflation) can impact negatively on the livelihoods of the poor.

Little research has been done, but there is a useful example from Tanzania. By using CGE model analysis, Kweka (2004) modelled the impact of the appreciation of the exchange rate on the poor and found that tourism growth could have significant negative effects on the non-tourism export economy, and hence on the welfare of farmers. There is little other evidence specifically for developing countries. In Australia, Adams and Parmenter (1995) quantify the effects of tourism on the industrial and regional structures of the economy. Their results show that traditional export sectors can be crowded out by the growth of international tourism. This analysis provides a further warning to be aware of the distinction between the – normally positive – 'impacts' of tourism (through pathways 1 and 2) and the 'net benefits' of tourism, which require an examination of all three pathways.

More positively, Lejárraga and Walkenhorst (2006) have identified the presence of foreign tourists within the national borders of a developing country as one of the key dynamic benefits of international tourism. Tourism can support the discovery of new products and exports. The sector provides a 'yellow brick road' to economic diversification whereby domestic entrepreneurs can experiment to see what goods and services appeal to the international market before having to enter the international export markets. Their regression analysis provides empirical evidence consistent with the notion that countries that have experienced an increase in tourism demand have also exhibited higher diversification of their exports over the same period. It is possible to see this trend in parts of Southeast Asia, like Hoi-An in central Vietnam. Family textile businesses that were producing entirely for the tourist market 15 years ago are now large textile export businesses with a small residual retail outlet in the destination, the only sign of their origins.

Bowen et al (1991) suggest that tourism-induced improvements in the Hawaiian marketing system may encourage the production of high-value, non-traditional agricultural products, and tourism may stimulate landscaping and other services based on agriculture which offset decreases in traditional agricultural activities.

The extent to which linkages are developed between the tourism industry and the rest of the economy is crucial in determining the externalities of the former on the other sectors. Analysing the impacts of enclave tourism in the Okavango Delta in Botswana, Mbaiwa (2000) suggests that tourism has had minimal economic impact on rural development mainly because it had weak linkages with the domestic economy, particularly agriculture (e.g. in 1999 tourism only contributed 0.5 per cent to agricultural output). Hence, an expansion of tourism activity in the Delta may not provide significant incentives for domestic resources to flow into the agricultural sector.

Tourism and agriculture

The agriculture sector experiences several dynamic externalities from tourist activity. This can have important poverty effects as agriculture employs a large share of the labour force in developing countries.

The agricultural supply chain provides a potentially important linkage between the tourist sector and the local economy. A significant proportion of the tourist studies literature examining this issue suggests that the relationship between tourism and food production is antagonistic. Researchers have often questioned whether tourism can utilize local agricultural produce, rather than simply import food for tourists. In addition, there is concern about competition for land, labour and capital between tourism and agriculture. The dynamic effects are strongest through the structure of product and factor markets (land resources, natural resources, labour markets). Table 6.2 summarizes some of the negative and positive impacts of tourism on agriculture that are found in the literature.

On the other hand, there are empirical studies that emphasize positive impacts. Knowd (2006) has suggested that, far from being antagonistic, agriculture and tourism share reciprocal interests in the attempt to strive for

Table 6.2 *The negative and positive impacts of tourism on agriculture*

Negative impacts of tourism on agriculture	Positive impacts of tourism on agriculture
Competition for land resources	Stimulation of agricultural development
Inflated land values	Increased profitability of agricultural production
Competition for labour resources	Creation of new market opportunities
Increased imports associated with foreign exchange leakages	Providing farmers with increased or supplementary income
Inflated food prices	
Changes in cropping patterns	
Decline in agricultural production	
Deterioration of the natural resource base	
Misdistribution of tourism benefits	

Source: Adapted from Meyer, 2006

sustainable development. Studies that have collected information from hotels generally find that a surprising amount of food is procured locally. Little evidence seems to confirm the assumption that higher quality hotels have a greater propensity to import food than other hotel categories or locally owned enterprises (Telfer and Wall, 2000). Telfer and Wall (1996) argue that the two sectors can be mutually reinforcing: tourism promotion focusing on agricultural products can boost demand, while agricultural promotion focusing on regional landscapes can lead to positive growth in tourism.

In Kenya, between 1968 and 1976, linkages between the tourism sector and domestic agriculture and food processing improved. The 70 per cent increase in tourist spending between 1971 and 1976 generated a 262 per cent increase in agricultural output. During this period the output of the food preparation industry expanded by 720 per cent. The figures are not adjusted for any differences in price changes between sectors. Yet, it is clear that real output in agriculture and food preparation undoubtedly expanded. This is a desirable result since over 70 per cent of Kenya's labour force was engaged in agriculture as recently as 1980 (Summary, 1987).

Dynamic effects experienced and captured in the local economy

Dynamic linkages are sometimes more visible in local areas. Local economic development is a recent field in tourism research, with the aim of locating comparative and competitive advantages of a local economy and building upon this – which can include certain explicit objectives such as a redistributive or pro-poor growth goal. Local economic development provides an understanding of how tourism fits in the local economic strategy.

In the past, economic development strategies generally, and local economic development specifically, have been agnostic about which economic sectors to support – simply working with the reality and potential facing each specific locality. However, tourism is emerging as of particular interest in some places, for four main reasons.

First, the identification of tourism as a key engine of change in the local economy by local stakeholders is becoming increasingly common. Tourism is often the economic sector that stimulates enthusiasm across a broad coalition of local stakeholders.

In South Africa, tourism has been identified by government as having an important role in transforming the (local) economy – nothing short of de-racializing the historically white-owned tourism sector. This is being attempted with the support of small, black businesses in a context where tourism enterprise is dominated by historically advantaged entrepreneurs (Rogerson, 2005b, 2007). To an extent, 'black' and 'white' are categories that imply 'poor' and 'affluent'. However, with the emergence of a black middle-class, many of these historic socio-economic categories are breaking down.

Second, local economic development approaches are particularly suited to regarding the destination as the most appropriate spatial unit of analysis. Tour operators, tourist product owners and tourists themselves tend to view tourism as a collection of destinations – and researchers are catching up with this reality. An important explanation for the lack of productive communication between tourism researchers and the private sector has been the fact that researchers have tended to either focus on the single hotel or lodge on the one hand, or the whole country on the other – neither of which are comfortable terrain for the tourism industry. Local economic development can help to adopt a middle way.

Third, strong local backward linkages are a characteristic of the tourism sector as outlined in Chapter 5. This means that identifying and strengthening these linkages is often an important research task in a tourist destination (Telfer and Wall, 1996). Local economic development has included a series of tools, such as local economic mapping and participatory VCA (Meyer-Stamer, 2004).

Finally, there is significant evidence in the literature that stakeholders in the locality do have a critical role in both encouraging tourism itself and, also, developing an enabling environment that spreads the benefits of tourism progressively within the locality and beyond. In particular, infrastructure, human resources and safety issues have an important influence on the attractiveness of tourist destinations and also the ability of the poor to access the tourism value chain, and it might be that such issues are more appropriately addressed at the local rather than the national level.

Tourism and long-term economic development

The tourism studies literature has tended to only look at the non-tourism economy where it has supply chain links with the tourism sector. In addition, the focus has been on the static – or immediate one-off – effects of tourism, rather than any more complicated, dynamic effects. When a hotel opens staff are appointed; visitors arrive; money is spent; goods are procured. Much of the tourism studies literature has not questioned two critical assumptions: a simple linear relationship between tourism and the rest of the economy, and an exclusive preoccupation with static effects.

For many researchers, the growth in tourist revenue and jobs is so self-evidently a 'good thing' for the broader economy that the link between tourism growth and economic development has not been explored. Other researchers, critical of tourism impacts, have focused their efforts on issues such as cultural contagion and social degeneration – well beyond the boundaries of an economic analysis.

However, some researchers have applied quantitative approaches (mainly regression analysis and CGE models) to understand the relationship between tourism – as a small sector of the economy – and the economic development of the country as a whole. This research is widening the horizons of thinking and has stimulated a vigorous and informed debate over the apparently most basic question, 'is tourism growth good for the economy?'

This is an important piece of the jigsaw regarding how tourism impacts on poor people. If the pro-poor impacts within tourism and related sectors in pathways 1 and 2 are undermined by what is happening in the rest of the economy, an apparently successful tourism development strategy may actually increase poverty. Conversely, if tourism growth has positive dynamic effects on the rest of the economy, the direct and indirect static benefits of a buoyant tourism sector may be reinforced by dynamic effects reverberating throughout the economy.

The evidence and diversity of views regarding the role of tourism in national economic development are illustrated in Table 6.3. The evidence based on CGE models and regression analysis shows that tourism is associated with growth in the long run and that there are positive effects on the national economy in terms of employment, economic growth and welfare, improving terms of trade and the potential to increase prosperity in rural areas. Algieri (2006) and Brau et al (2003) provide evidence that specialization in tourism is associated with higher economic growth rates considered as a function of the national per-capita income. On the other hand, tourism may also result in lower growth in the form of reduced agricultural and manufacturing output; mass migration from rural areas with increasing urban unemployment; and poor long-term growth prospects due to low productivity growth.

There has been a lot of analysis but so far with few clear results. A key finding is that the sustained long-run effects of tourism will depend on a host of other factors.

A brief synthesis is as follows:

- Most of the empirical regression analyses conclude that tourism boosts national economic growth, although it can clearly make economic growth more volatile. The most pessimistic analyses are generally derived from

Table 6.3 *Tourism and economic development*

Issue	Finding	Source
Economic development		
Does tourism bring economic as well as environmental and social and cultural costs to Middle East and North African destinations?	Applying a CGE model, it is concluded that tourism has ambiguous net benefits for domestic welfare. Under certain conditions (e.g. when tourism is less labour intensive than agriculture) welfare gains from improved terms of trade caused by tourism growth can be eliminated by the rise in unemployment rate as a consequence of declining agricultural output versus increase of tourism, with negative impact on domestic welfare.	Sahli and Nowak, 2005
What is the impact of tourism growth on Cyprus, Malta and Mauritius?	Applying a CGE model, an increase in tourist demand has positive macro-economic impacts. GDP increases and welfare rises. Employment effects are positive – although not calculated for Mauritius where unemployment level is negligible already. Tourism has a positive impact on agriculture and fishing sectors and allows rural populations to become more prosperous without having to migrate to the towns.	Sinclair et al, 2004
What is the relationship between tourism demand and GDP volatility in the US?	Applying a regression analysis, a significantly positive relationship between international tourism receipts as a percentage of total exports and volatility in the annual GDP growth rate is detected. +1% in US per capita GDP increases tourism demand to an average destination by approximately 1.46%.	Brakke, 2005
How does tourism affect the growth of small countries?	Undertook an econometric analysis based on time-series of 25 developing countries. It is corroborated that the opportunity cost of tourism specialization is proportional to a country's size so it is beneficial for small countries to specialize in tourism. Although manufacturing has higher labour productivity, tourism economies can grow sustainably over the long term.	Algieri, 2006
Does tourism cause economic growth, or vice versa, in Korea?	Through application of a time-series method of causality testing – where both short-run dynamic relations and long-run equilibrium conditions are tested – the tourism-led growth hypothesis is questioned. In fact it appears that economic expansion leads to tourist growth, rather than the other way around.	Oh, 2005
Does tourist specialization stifle technological change and, thus, long-run economic growth in 13 OECD countries?	A general equilibrium model is applied to demonstrate that the effects of specialization in tourism – a 'less progressive' sector in the sense of demonstrating slower labour productivity and 'learning by doing' growth than other sectors – are more than off-set by the shift in terms of trade that move in their favour. In other words, there is no conflict between static and dynamic comparative advantage – so that the long-run growth of countries with a comparative advantage in tourism will not suffer from a specialization in tourism.	Lanza et al, 2002

Issue	Finding	Source
What is the impact of tourism on growth, and its stability, in Hawaii?	An econometric model identified the impact of tourism on growth 1953–1970. Results revealed that in the absence of tourism growth personal income would have been 17% lower – an average figure of 6.87% compared with the actual 7.99% per year. Hence, tourism increases the variability of growth as it is captured by the increase of the coefficient of variation of growth by 21%	Ghali, 1976
What is the impact of tourism specialization on economic growth for small countries across 114 countries?	An econometric analysis regressing growth rate of groups of countries (small tourism countries; Organisation for Economic Co-operation and Development (OECD) countries; oil exporting countries; LDCs, etc.) between 1985 and 1995 concluded that tourism specialization is beneficial to small countries. Also small tourism countries (countries with less than 1 million population and more than 10% international tourism receipts to GDP) have less volatile growth than comparable small, non-tourism countries. Whether this growth is sustainable in the long run depends upon whether pessimism about poor productivity growth in tourism is offset by optimism about positive terms of trade effects.	Brau et al, 2003
What is the contribution of tourism in Mauritius, Zimbabwe and South Africa?	Tourism is an important and growing sector, although perhaps less so than the most enthusiastic estimates. Tourism damage is often overstated, and it is not so different from other sectors as it is often stated.	Page, 1999
What is the contribution of tourism to the Hong Kong economy?	An I–O model is applied to quantify the total (direct and indirect) economic contribution of tourism to the Hong Kong economy. Over time, the total income generated by tourism as a percentage of GDP has been increasing despite a declining ratio of tourism expenditure to GDP. This is due to the decreasing leakage of tourism. The increase in the contribution to employment is even more marked than the increase in contribution to GDP.	Lin and Sung, 1984
Exports		
Does international tourism 'crowd out' traditional export sectors in Australia?	It is concluded that international tourism crowds out traditional export sectors – such as agriculture and mining – in the Queensland economy. This has important macro-economic policy implications because it suggests that additional tourism will hinder, not assist, efforts to reduce the current account deficit. Domestic welfare can be increased by taking the opportunity to tax tourists.	Adams and Parmenter, 1995
Can tourism lead to de-industrialization and 'Dutch disease'?	The application of a two-sector, dynamic framework suggests that tourism growth tends to improve welfare in the short and medium term, but can be 'immiserating' in the long run if the loss in welfare from de-industrialization is larger than the gain from the terms of trade improvement. The 'Dutch disease' literature refers to supply shocks, such as the discovery of natural resources; this analysis suggests a tourism boom can generate the same negative effects.	Chao et al, 2006

Table 6.3 *Tourism and economic development (continued)*

Issue	Finding	Source
Taxation		
How has tourism interacted with globalization reforms in Indonesia?	Using a CGE model based on a SAM, it is found that tourism amplifies the positive aspects of globalization (fall in domestic prices and a rise in comparative advantage, production, employment and GDP) and, at the same time, reduces its adverse effects (reducing tariffs and tax associated with globalization reduces government revenues. This is compensated by foreign tourist arrivals, which allow governments to maintain their programmes without facing fiscal problems). Tourism improves GDP, employment and reduces the trade deficit.	Sugiyarto et al, 2002
Does tax collected from tourism exceed the public investments required?	Governments simultaneously regard tourism as a major charge to the budget and a 'cash cow'. The evidence suggests that tourism can generate sufficient taxes to more than compensate for public investments.	Christie and Crompton, 2001
Income distribution		
What are the distributional implications of tourism growth in Tanzania?	Applying a CGE model, it is shown that tourism expansion has a substantial positive impact on the economy by increasing GDP, total welfare and exports. However, rural households do not benefit because their livelihoods are dependent upon the export of agricultural produce – which is deleteriously affected by appreciation in the real exchange rate resulting from a surge of foreign exchange due to international tourism. With an improvement in rural infrastructure and taxation of tourists the beneficial impacts of tourism can be amplified, resulting in rural households increasing welfare twice as much as urban households. Tourism, in itself, is ineffective at reducing poverty unless it is part of a deliberate effort to improve infrastructure and distribution mechanisms.	Kweka, 2004
What is the distributional impact of tourism in Brazil?	A CGE model that explicitly examines the distributional impact of tourism and outlines the different 'channels' for pro-poor impact. The analysis revealed that direct wages were the most important pro-poor channel and, although tourist demand increased prices in the domestic economy, this mainly impacted upon the local elite rather than the poor. The failure of government spending to reach the poor is striking.	Blake et al, 2008

theoretical models that are based more on researchers' assumptions and less on actual country development trajectories than in the econometric studies. There is sufficient evidence, however, to question an assumption that tourism development inevitably equates to national economic development.

- Divergent findings in the various analyses may reflect differences in the time frame chosen. Several analyses suggest that tourism will have a positive impact in the short run, but that this is not sustainable into the long run, principally due to low productivity growth in tourism.
- Tourist development is more appropriate for some countries than others due to geographic determinism. For instance, small, tourist-dependent island states or very poor countries may have fewer options aside from encouraging tourism – and less industry and agriculture to damage from 'Dutch disease'[1] – compared with a large and diversified economy. On the other hand, inter-sector linkages between the tourism and non-tourism economy should be deeper in more sophisticated economies.
- Several studies emphasize the role of tourism as a source of taxation for government. This can have powerful positive effects on the poor where government has a redistributive policy programme. The efficiency, magnitude and pro-poor potential of tourism taxes are a feature of several analyses.
- The few analyses with a distributional focus suggest that a policy of simply growing tourism as quickly as possible is insufficient to guarantee pro-poor growth. The poor can benefit from tourism at a national level, but this requires thoughtful and deliberate complementary policies – often outside the tourist sector.

The implications of this brief overview are important. Researchers concerned with the distributional consequences of tourism, whatever their particular geographical or niche focus, ought to engage with these issues in order to contribute to the public policy debate. Under certain circumstances, buoyant tourism growth may be harmful for large numbers of vulnerable households, such as farmers, or for the welfare of the population as a whole. Even though tourism is a significant part of the economy of many poor countries, researchers cannot simply conclude that, because tourism is big, it must be developmentally benign. In fact, the size and buoyant growth of tourism can – under specific circumstances – create the conditions that actually harm the welfare of poor people.

Finally, while econometric evidence shows that tourism development contributes to economic growth in low- and middle-income countries, there are a host of factors that help to improve the positive effects of tourism and mitigate the negative effects. Tourism may not be inherently good or bad as it depends on the complementary factors such as better infrastructure, education and safety that ought to be key elements of a tourism development policy (Eugenio-Martín et al, 2004). Lejárraga and Walkenhorst (2006) identify improving the business climate; improving human capital (including the participation of women in the economy); institutions and openness to trade as key determinants to benefiting from tourism.

Note

1 Dutch disease is an economic condition which refers to the negative consequences arising from any large increase in foreign currency. Dutch disease is normally associated with a natural resource discovery, but can result from any large increase in foreign exchange, including foreign aid, foreign direct investment – or even tourism receipts. The theory is that a large inflow of foreign currency will de-industrialize the economy by raising the exchange rate, making manufacturing less competitive, and the public sector will become entangled with business interests.

7
Impacts of Different Types of Tourism

Assumptions about how different types of tourism generate completely different impacts on the local economy are rife. These assumptions influence government policy about tourism marketing and development. But this review has found an extreme paucity of data in this critical area for policy makers. First, very little tourism analysis is actually disaggregated by type of tourist. Most analyses are either for some 'average' tourist, or are specific to just one product, such as tourists that use campsites, or safari lodges, or beach resorts. Second, there is even less analysis that makes comparisons between different segments across the tourist sector. Some reports contain scanty information on how expenditure patterns differ by type of tourist. Beyond that, the field is empty. There does not appear to have been any attempt to rigorously assess and compare the impact of different types of tourist in the same destination using the same evaluation methodology. This is remarkable given how many policy documents give clear policy preference to certain segments.

As Sinclair (1998, p17) declared:

> *It is evident that policy-makers in developing countries need to pay more attention to the issue of the segments of the tourism market that they wish to attract; for example, the costs and benefits of low price, high volume, mass tourism relative to high price, low volume, special interest tourism.*

In Kenya, analysis has shown the higher expenditure per capita, but somewhat smaller multiplier, associated with safari tourism relative to beach tourism (Sinclair, 1991). The growth of beach tourism has reduced average foreign currency receipts per capita but increased the impact on the non-tourist economy. In addition, safari tourism has other associated costs (such as infrastructure maintenance) that needed to be taken into account in cost benefit analysis of different segments. So, the policy question facing several East African states is what mix of safari/beach/other tourism should be offered to the international market to maximize the benefits for the host country. We think our analysis of the Kilimanjaro and safari value chains in northern Tanzania may have been the first attempt to undertake a comparative assessment of these two distinct value chains (Mitchell et al, 2009). Without this information about the scale, trends, yield, multiplier and pro-poor impact of different segments, it is difficult to see on what basis policy makers can plan tourist development in countries offering more than one product.

Archer and Fletcher (1996) demonstrate that certain types of visitors to the Seychelles are economically more beneficial than others. Higher spending tourists may have a greater economic impact per visitor than others. Tourists from Germany, for example, accounted for only 10.4 per cent of foreign visitors, but their expenditure contributed over 13 per cent of the tourism-related employment. Africans accounted for 20.9 per cent of all tourists but generated only 16.8 per cent of tourism-generated jobs. This information does not reveal anything about differential impact per tourist dollar spent, or the differential cost of attracting the marginal extra tourist.

Whilst it is known that different categories of tourist spend divergent amounts of money per trip or per day, it is not clear what the effects of these differences are. For instance, the Tanzanian tourism master plan indicates that conference, business and recreational tourists spend an average in country of US$600, $900 and $1000 per head per trip respectively (CHL Consulting, 2002). However, from the foregoing information, the policy response is not obvious – other than to conclude that encouraging recreational tourism might be an effective strategy to maximize international tourist expenditure. It is quite likely, on the basis of the studies reviewed as part of this exercise, that the geographical and distributional effects of $1000 spent on holiday in Kilimanjaro are completely different from $900 spent during a business trip to the capital Dar es Salaam. It is quite clear that simply maximizing tourism receipts is not necessarily pro-poor, indeed it might not even be pro-development. The implication of this is that the scramble for increasing numbers of high-spending tourists, without considering the economic and distributional effects of this expenditure, may be undermining the chances for pro-poor growth.

Dwyer (2005) points out that which segment is 'high yield' is not necessarily the same as knowing which segment is 'high spending'. He uses five different measures of economic yield, and the ranking of high-yield and low-yield markets varies according to which measure is used. He concludes that neither expenditure nor GDP contribution are reliable proxies for assessing net benefit of different market segments. As a result, targeting 'high-yield' markets may not be an optimal strategy either for individual operators or for destination managers. 'The economic impacts depend upon the tourist's pattern of expenditure; that is, the types of goods and services purchased, not just its volume' (Dwyer, 2005, p10). However, in applying a similar conceptual approach to an analysis of tourism types in New Zealand, Becken and Butcher (2004) find that different measures of yield do not produce significant differences in the ranking of different tourist segments.

Table 7.1 *High and low linkages around cultural and beach products*

	Cultural tourism	Package beach tourism	Business tourism	Eco-tourism
High out-of-pocket spending in the local economy	Laos (Luang Prabang) Ethiopia (outside Addis Ababa)	The Gambia	Central Vietnam	Tanzania (northern circuit safari)
Low out-of-pocket spending in the local economy	Cambodia	Tunisia, Cape Verde	Ghana, Ethiopia	Tanzania (Mount Kilimanjaro)

Source: Ashley, 2006a; Mitchell and Coles, 2009; ODI and UNDP, 2009; Mitchell and Faal, 2008; UNCTAD, 2007; Mitchell and Le Chi, 2007; Coles and Mitchell, 2009; Mitchell et al, 2009

Table 7.1 compares four studies on the incomes that flow to the poor in four distinct destinations. It shows that strong linkages with the local economy are not predetermined by the type of tourism, because there are examples of cultural tourism with high and low linkages, and examples of beach tourism with high and low linkages.

In The Gambia, Mitchell and Faal (2008) show that a 4 star package holiday costs over 25 per cent more than a 3 star package. However, out-of-pocket spend per tourist differs little between tourists in 2, 3, 4 and 5 star accommodation, as shown in Figure 7.1, so upmarket tourists are not necessarily better for poor people in the local economy.

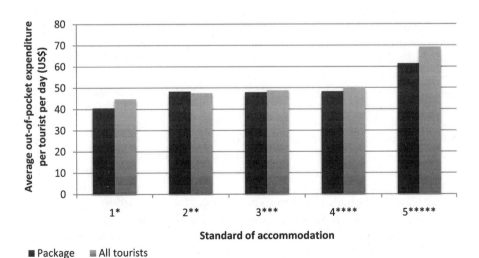

Source: Mitchell and Faal, 2008

Figure 7.1 *Out of pocket expenditure by hotel rating*

This analysis questions the assumption that a higher quality of tourist product necessarily brings any additional benefits to the local community. In addition, a central tenant of tourism development in The Gambia, that tourist activity should spread beyond the enclave on the Atlantic coast, to strengthen links with the poor hinterland, is questioned:

> *This study finds little evidence to support the view that small, up-country tourist product will necessarily be more pro-poor than the current product. The key mechanisms for poverty reduction through tourism are in activities like staffing and supplying large hotels and restaurants and the operation of craft markets, excursions and local transportation facilities. If product development focuses upon dispersing the tourism product across the country in a shotgun approach there is a danger that the mechanisms which link the poor to the benefits of tourism will not reach a critical mass for viability and, therefore, will not take place. In this sense, mass tourism could be more accessible to the poor than niche ecotourism operations'* (Mitchell and Faal, 2008).

In Luang Prabang, Laos, Ashley (2006a) found that upmarket, mid-range and budget tourists differed substantially in their expenditure per day within the destination, but there was less difference in the income flows that reached the poor per tourist, directly and indirectly. The high-end tourist spends almost three times as much per trip as the budget tourist. But incomes reaching the poor directly and indirectly, amounted to 30 per cent of budget tourist spend, compared to 17 per cent of upmarket tourist spend. This is because the main difference in trip expenditure between high-end and budget tourists is for accommodation, of which a low share reaches the poor. Income to the poor per tourist trip therefore only varied from \$35 for budget tourists to \$59 for high-end tourists – a much smaller differential than the threefold difference in total expenditure.

Scheyvens (2002) suggests that backpacker tourists can stimulate more significant multiplier effects, as people with little capital or training can pro- vide desired services or products. Backpackers have a demand for local goods and services, rather than imported goods and, in comparison with large- scale development, backpacker tourism needs only cheap, simply constructed accommodation requiring relatively low investment. Owner construction also lowers this initial cost. The same applies to cheap restaurants frequented by backpackers, which also have low entry costs (Hampton, 1999).

Lengefeld and Stewart's (2004) review of all-inclusive resorts seeks to question the widely held assumption that they do not benefit the local econ- omy. The research assessed seven all-inclusive resorts in three Caribbean countries. Each resort created between 190 and 450 jobs. The 3–4 star all- inclusive resorts typically create 1 job per room (compared with 0.5–0.7 jobs per room in conventional hotels), while 5 star all-inclusive resorts typically generate 1.5–2 jobs per room (compared with 1 job per room in conventional

5 star hotels). In all but one of the resorts surveyed less than 10 per cent of the jobs were seasonal. It should be noted that data averages are influenced by Sandals Resorts – which is probably the most progressive example of all-inclusive resorts in the Caribbean.

Travelwatch (2006) examines the literature related to economic contribution of all-inclusive resorts in the Caribbean region. Studies to date have illustrated that all-inclusive resorts can have a more beneficial impact on the local economy than previously assumed. Intuition suggests that all-inclusive resorts create more jobs in the hotel, but fewer jobs outside the hotel – because the aim of the all-inclusive model is to provide all services on site and to avoid tourists having to carry cash to pay for goods and services. On average the researchers found that there were between 2 and 4 indirect jobs created in the supply chain, for each all-inclusive resort job. Unfortunately the research did not complete a full comparison of this effect with non-all-inclusive resorts. Nevertheless, it did succeed in demonstrating the substantial positive local economic impact that all-inclusive resorts can achieve.

In Bali, the largest hotels employed 2 per room compared with 'home stay' accommodation figures of 0.47 per room, although this excludes unpaid family members (Rodenburg, 1980). If investment per room and investment per job created are used as indicators, then the largest hotels have the highest cost per room, so that smaller projects generate more rooms and more jobs for a given unit of investment.

The lack of research attention paid to domestic tourism in developing countries could be based upon the dated assumption that developing countries are not source markets for tourists. It could also partly be due to the lack of readily available information on domestic tourists, who sleep in homes, do not pass border controls and are less 'visible' than foreigners. This leads to an over-reliance on international visitor data (see Goodwin, 2006a). In many developing economies, not only are most tourists domestic and regional, but so is tourist expenditure. In 2003, domestic tourists in Ecuador contributed approximately $217 million towards tourism receipts, compared to the $406 million contributed by international tourists (Fries et al, 2006). In much of Southeast Asia, domestic and regional tourism represent the bulk of tourist expenditure in many destinations. In tourist destinations like Da Nang in central Vietnam the extent to which the world is changing becomes apparent. A recent tourist value chain study revealed that two-thirds of tourist expenditure is domestic, with the fastest growth in the international market being China and the highest daily spend being from tourists from Singapore (Mitchell and Le Chi, 2007). In sub-Saharan Africa, we have quantified the scale of domestic business tourism and found it to be very significant in terms of total expenditure, and more so in terms of pro-poor impact, compared with international business tourism.

Understanding the impact of domestic tourism in emerging markets is important because many of the dynamic effects of tourism (both positive and negative) may be quite different from international tourism. Domestic tourism will not result in foreign exchange 'shocks' to the economy, but neither will it result in the opportunity for local entrepreneurs to learn what they are good at producing from the international market. Pathway 3 could look very different. It is also possible that domestic tourist expenditure may be more closely linked to locally produced goods and services – so that pathway 2 is more significant.

It is clear from this short section that, as tourism researchers, we have failed to provide policy makers in developing countries with adequate analysis of the diverse impacts of different types of tourism from contrasting source markets. We know enough to be confident that relying on 'old style' indicators such as international arrival numbers and average tourist spend are inadequate. These often generate inaccurate, if not misleading, measures of how much tourism is benefiting the local economy and poor people within it. We are also inching our way towards a much clearer understanding of the measures which will generate options that will give policy makers meaningful choices about an alternative future. As researchers and practitioners, we have a responsibility to provide a better service to policy makers and, ultimately, the resource poor.

8
Methods for Assessing the Impacts of Tourism on Poverty

Previous chapters of this book illustrate the diversity of evidence available on the impacts of tourism on poverty. Not only the data, but the methods used to generate them, vary enormously. This diversity undermines the comparability, which is one of the most significant obstacles to presenting a coherent synthesis on this topic.

This chapter reflects on the various methodologies used, their strengths, weaknesses, and relevance for answering the key policy questions about poverty impacts of tourism. It mirrors the categorization of four types of literature that was presented in Chapter 1, namely research that:

1 assesses the economic effects of tourism activities on the economy;
2 describes the size of the tourism sector;
3 measures impacts of tourism on poor people or local economies in tourist destinations;
4 develops and enhances the tourist sectors' growth and competitiveness.

In each of these categories, the main assessment methods used are reviewed below. It has to be recognized at the outset that sometimes life does not fit easily into neat boxes – and so some methods straddle some of the categories.

Assessing the effects of tourism activities on the economy

I–O models
Input–output tables are based on national accounts data and provide a quant-itative description of the inter-sector linkages in the economy. Such linkages are captured by a matrix, which describes the units of additional outputs needed from each sector of the economy to satisfy one extra unit of final demand in a certain sector.

Researchers have used these tables to calculate the effects of an increase in final demand in tourism on each of the productive sectors and hence on the entire economy. Combining visitor spending with input–output analysis allows researchers to estimate the impact of changes in tourist demand on the economy. Thus they can estimate the contribution of direct and indirect tourism to macro-economic aggregates such as output, incomes, jobs and sales, and to generate estimates of multipliers.

The beauty of this approach is the prominence it gives to inter-sectoral linkages, which as we have seen, are key to understanding the poverty impacts of tourism. In Egypt, for instance, input–output analysis suggests that hotels and restaurants (most of what officially constitutes the tourism sector) account for only 30–40 per cent of total tourist expenditure. An analysis of inter-sector linkages suggests that, in reality, tourist expenditure is responsible for up to three times the volume of activity reported in official figures (Tohamy and Swinscoe, 2000).

However, the results of I–O models tend to remain within a technical *milieu*. They are rarely used by policy makers and, on the occasions that they are, may be misinterpreted.[1] I–O models in isolation consider neither distributional nor dynamic effects. For example, substitution effects will occur when prices change (meaning that when the costs of goods and services change, so do our spending patterns), but these are not modelled. According to Ennew (2003), this weakness has resulted in several practical examples where predictions of tourist expenditure, in response to changes in demand, have been wildly inaccurate.

While estimating the magnitude of linkages to specific sectors of the non-tourism economy is useful, policy makers need more information on how the increase in tourism demand that generates those linkages should be created, and on how the linkage impacts are distributed. Thus the value of input–output analysis is as a descriptive method of quantifying links between tourism

Table 8.1 *Assessment of I–O models*

Positive
Highlights the scale and nature of linkages between tourism and other sectors of the economy
Enables measurement of second and further round economic effects of tourism
Can be used widely, as input–output tables are often available 'off the shelf'
Generate data needed for other methods, such as equilibrium models

Negative
Based on inaccurate assumptions about how the economy works; cannot allow for dynamic effects
Attempts to construct dynamic input–output models have been constrained by prohibitive data requirements; few such models have been attempted
Beyond informing policy makers that tourism makes a larger contribution to the economy than official figures suggest, the policy contribution of input–output analysis has been limited
Does not explicitly consider distributional issues

Which pathway, which poor?
Pathway 2: The size of indirect effects
On its own, it does not include any measurement of how benefits are distributed among different groups of people

---

and the rest of the economy. This is important, but only as a stepping-stone towards our goal of understanding the links between tourism and poor people.

Regression analysis

Regression analysis is a statistical tool applied in the social sciences to analyse the relationship (and possibly the causality) between a dependent variable and independent (or explanatory) variable(s). Real data are then used to test the extent to which the explanatory variables account for observed changes in the dependent variable.

A simple linear regression model involves one dependent (y-axis) and one explanatory (x-axis) variable. To measure the relationship between these two variables, data are necessary to estimate the intercept and slope (i.e. parameters $\beta1$ and $\beta2$) for the 'best fit' line that describes the relationship between two variables. Econometrics is a technique to compute this line of 'best fit'.

However, in the real world of economics, for each dependent (or endogenous) variable there tend to be several explanatory factors. For example, individuals' incomes may depend on their level of education (years of schooling), intelligence, social class, etc. Hence, econometric analysis usually takes the form of a multiple linear regression model, to which matrix algebra is applied, in order to estimate the relationship between variables.

Regression analysis has been used to explore the relationship between tourism growth and macro-economic growth. It provides a means of integrating

Table 8.2 *Assessment of regression analysis*

Positive
Allows the analysis of huge amounts of data (which are usually readily available for most countries)
Empirical data are used to measure relationships between variables, rather than being assumed by researchers
Outputs of regression analysis can be used to determine the parameters of equilibrium models
Encourages researchers to look for findings that can be generalized, rather than the focus on large numbers of – often highly specific – case studies

Negative
Determining the direction of causality – rather than just a relationship between two variables – can be problematic
Cross-country analyses often suffer from the problems of controlling for unobserved heterogeneity across countries, that may bias the results
If welfare is considered in regression analysis it is normally not disaggregated between households at different levels of income

Which pathway, which poor?
All types of impact, depending on how it is modelled
It is most often used to explore impacts arising from all three pathways, in terms of the relationship between tourism growth and long-term trends in macro economic growth
It rarely focuses on distributional or poverty issues
Results for the domestic sector as a whole would not distinguish between households in a tourist destination and those outside

---

data from a vast range of countries – 150 countries in some literature reviewed here – which would simply not be possible using other methods. However, attributing the direction of causality can be problematic (evidenced by the debate about whether tourism causes macro-economic growth or vice versa).

With one notable exception in Namibia (see Bandyopadhyay et al, 2004), which assessed the relationship between participation in local wildlife tourism institutions ('conservancies') and household welfare, the regression analysis examined in this review has been applied to macro-economic growth variables with no distributional focus.

This focus on big picture trends, comparisons and macro-economic variables adds a useful balance to those perspectives that focus heavily on small-scale, pro-poor impact at the risk of neglecting the long-term growth implications of tourism arrivals. But in isolation, these big picture correlations are of course insufficient for understanding poverty impacts.

SAMs

SAMs build on input–output tables to develop a matrix that takes account of sectors, commodities, primary factors and households by type. A SAM defines the monetary transactions between economic actors. In doing this, it reveals the relationship between the different economic actors and gives an overview of the socio-economic structure – thus linking the two normally distinct social and economic domains.

As an example, a SAM was built to assess nature tourism in northeast KwaZulu-Natal (Mullins and Mulder, 2003). The impact of a change in nature tourism spending inside the study area was tracked in terms of its effect on sector activities, factor payments (capital, labour), enterprises, household income and employment creation. Disaggregation within each category enabled a specific focus on impacts on particular groups of people. Returns to labour

Table 8.3 *Assessment of SAMs*

Positive

SAMs are the most complete static representation of the economy, combining the inter-sector focus of input–output analysis with a strong distributional focus

SAMs cross the divide between economic and social concerns by integrating two sets of statistics

SAMs provide inputs for other more complex models and are increasingly available

Negative

On their own, they do not incorporate dynamic effects

As with other models, their value depends on the validity of the assumptions involved, and their policy utility on the level of disaggregation possible

Which pathway, which poor?

SAMs can be used to analyse impacts on specific poor groups, such as unskilled workers, or low-income households – in terms of direct and indirect effects (Pathways 1 and 2)

The geographic scale of poor groups will depend on the coverage of the SAM, which is often national but can also cover a sub-national region

---

were divided by skill level (unskilled, semi-skilled and skilled) and returns to capital included returns to small enterprises and local communities. Impacts were assessed inside the immediate study region, and in the wider economy of KwaZulu-Natal. The results showed the relatively high flow of benefits to unskilled and semi-skilled workers and small enterprise, the low level of linkages with non-tourism sectors within the local economy, and the relatively higher level of linkage with the rest of the KwaZulu-Natal economy. Similarly to the methodology used by Turpie et al (2004), an important adaptation from a generic SAM was that each different type of tourism was treated as a sector on its own, so that differentiated assumptions could be entered into the matrix.

SAMs have been shown to be a very useful tool, though in a limited number of cases, for assessing direct and indirect flows from tourism across a destination, with a strong distributional focus.

CGE models

CGE models are a tool used to simulate the circular flows of goods and services within an economic system of producers, consumers, markets, government and financial institutions. The essence of the model is to predict, through numerical simulation approach, how changes ('shocks') affect the economy, under the assumption that price adjustments and factor mobility enable the product and factor markets in the economy to return to equilibrium following the shocks.

CGE modelling has been developed specifically to address the weakness of 'old' approaches to the evaluation of tourism's economic impacts (Dwyer, 2005). They have been applied in international trade and agricultural and environmental economics for many years – but only applied to tourism since 1995 in a move pioneered by the Nottingham Business School. CGE models have been used to explore macro-economic impacts of tourism in a way that goes beyond the capacity of static input–output models. Complex feedback effects, such as the relationship between accelerated globalization and increased tourism demand in Indonesia, have additionally been entered into CGE models (for example, Sugiyarto et al, 2002). CGE models are also able to measure the possibility that tourism can 'crowd out' previous economic activities (Copeland, 1991; Dwyer et al, 2000).

CGE modelling can be particularly useful in facilitating analysis of tourism policy-related issues. Paradoxically, then, these research methods are rarely used by development practitioners or public policy makers in developing countries – possibly because their application is still relatively recent. In addition, the models require considerable data to build (Dwyer et al, 2000; Dwyer, 2005), and if data are lacking, assumptions need to be made based on data from comparable alternative locations.

CGE modelling has traditionally looked at all households as a single category and assessed welfare changes for this aggregate category. This is obviously not particularly helpful to inform a PPT approach. But if linked to household surveys using social accounting matrices, finer distributional analysis is possible. More sophisticated regression and CGE modelling approaches are

Table 8.4 *Assessment of CGE models*

Positive

Capture dynamic affects – feedback mechanisms, substitution affects resulting from price changes etc.

Can be used to model the impact of different policy scenarios

Analyses can measure how much different types of household are affected by tourism, and also how these costs and benefits are transmitted

Negative

Although it is possible to create dynamic equilibrium models, they are highly complex (most models to date are static)

Findings of modelling exercises crucially rest on the kind of assumptions used to describe the relationship between the variables in the economy; local level data are often lacking

While some disaggregation is possible, it is unlikely to reach the level of detail for exploring the full range of pro-poor flows, beneficiaries and influencing factors that meso or micro studies can cover

Which pathway, which poor?

CGE models are particularly useful for analysing certain kinds of dynamic impacts relating to changes in macro-economic variables over time (pathway 3). They also cover pathways 1 and 2

Equilibrium analysis can examine the impact of tourism on unskilled labour or low-income households

Models are unlikely to categorize households geographically according to whether they are inside or outside the tourism destination

---

now emerging (e.g. Blake et al, 2008), which estimate tourism impacts on specific categories of household by income. This work is notable as the only example found that covers all three of the pathways in the conceptual model while including analysis of distributional flows to poor households.

CGE models are complex and are only as good as the data and assumptions on which they are built. But they offer an important way forward in assessing all three types of pathway by which tourism can impact on poverty, particularly when they integrate distributional analysis for different types of households. Sinclair et al (2006) identified three main areas of development for CGE models analysis: further research on dynamic analysis; incorporation of more micro-economic information into CGE models; and further modelling for policy analysis. All three of these will assist in strengthening our understanding of poverty impacts, particularly pathway 3, and their policy implications.

Describing the size of the tourism sector

TSAs

TSAs seek to present information on the economic contribution of tourism to the macro-economy using an internationally acceptable accounting framework, concepts, classifications and definitions. Although the literature echoes with claims that tourism satellite accounts measure the economic impact of tourism, they do not. Satellite accounts measure the size of tourism as an area of economic activity.

TSAs have been promoted vigorously by the UNWTO since a conference on tourism statistics held in 1991. Among developing and emerging economies, they have been implemented in Namibia, China with Hong Kong and Macau, Romania, Russian Federation, Greece, Egypt, Trinidad & Tobago, Caribbean, Montenegro, Kerala, Croatia, Algarve, South Africa, Tanzania and Malaysia (WTTC and OE, 2006). The limited uptake is partly because they are expensive to produce, requiring teams of researchers to set up a 'shadow' version of the national accounts.

TSAs deliver a 'better' (i.e. bigger) estimation of the size of the tourism economy than the international standard system of national accounts (SNA) because they use expenditure data to assess the true scope of tourism spending and input–output tables to assess the flow of tourist expenditure throughout the economy (see Frechtling, 1999; WTO, 2000; Brændvang et al, 2001; Virola et al, 2001; WTO, 2001; West and Jackson, 2004; Fan and Oosterhaven, 2005).

Pao (2005) identifies some tensions in the application of TSAs between the UNWTO that is encouraging tourism satellite accounts to be applied universally and fully consistent with the concepts and principles of SNA. In contrast, WTTC tends to use TSAs to emphasize the large scale of the contribution of tourism to economic development and to promote tourism expansion.

TSAs have many of the same weaknesses as I–O models. That is, they are static and ignore feedback effects. Because resources like land, labour and capital required by an expanding tourism sector would normally have some alternative productive use, the net effect of tourism growth will almost always be more muted than the gross effect that input–output tables and TSAs measure. But they have other weaknesses too. The volume of data required is a weakness given the contexts of limited institutional capacity. Sharma and Olsen (2005) argue for a more 'bottom up' approach, in which stakeholders identify those parts of the WTO approach to satellite accounts they most need, so as to boost relevance and feasibility of the process. Even with a trimmed version, however, it can also be argued that setting satellite accounts as the goal diverts attention away from data that would be more useful for modelling policy options and distributional impacts.

The policy utility of TSAs is at the same time their greatest policy asset and weakness. TSAs are useful to demonstrate to host governments the importance of the tourism economy. However, precisely because the output is a few aggregate numbers, they are not useful for providing the disaggregated analysis that developmental decision making requires. Knowing that tourism really accounts for, say, 5 per cent of the national economy rather than the 2 per cent derived from the national accounts tells decision makers little in terms of who benefits from tourism, which components of the industry deliver greatest impact, or what policy environment could grow the sector or change the pattern of growth.

TSAs have been highly effective at getting an important message to policy makers – tourism is, indeed, more significant than represented in the national accounts. However, they can be regarded as an expensive way of answering a

Table 8.5 *Assessment of TSAs*

Positive
Overcome the failure of national accounts to recognize the size of contribution of the tourism sector
Organize information on the effects of tourist activity in a way that is consistent with the 1993 system of national accounts
Encourage the use of standard terms and definition internationally, that would facilitate cross-country comparisons if more developing countries had adopted satellite accounts

Negative
Provide only a static snapshot of the size of the tourism industry
Provide no insight on the determinants of size, distribution of benefits, or impacts of policy scenarios
Expensive and time-consuming to produce
Caught between the need to stick with supply-side definitions for comparability with SNA, and need for demand-led definitions of tourism – the result is a range of measures, many of which are not legitimately comparable with SNA, and which are not fully understood by users

Which pathway, which poor?
TSAs draw on analysis of inter-sectoral linkages (pathway 2) but are not used to answer questions about the nature of those linkages
TSAs do not consider distributional issues

---

question that few people are asking – namely, what is the size of the tourism economy?

Measuring the impact of tourism on poor people or local economies in tourist destinations

Livelihoods analysis
A livelihoods analysis approach is often used to assess smaller scale, more rural and community-based tourism activities from the perspective of local people. Typically this involves a participatory rural appraisal methodology in conjunction with analysis of more quantitative data. Livelihoods analysis considers financial capital but also calculates other forms of capital (social, natural, human, physical), and looks at both positive and negative impacts (Jamieson et al, 2004).

Livelihoods analysis has been applied to the tourism sector mainly in the appraisal of community-based tourism and ecotourism projects. It is used extensively by non-governmental organizations (NGOs). It is particularly appropriate for use in rural areas where wage income is just one element of livelihood security, and other activities and assets are also of critical importance.

For instance, in a review of community-owned tourism enterprises in Caprivi in northern Namibia, the analysis revealed that only a limited number of jobs were created and these were poorly remunerated. However, the livelihoods analysis went beyond this and took into account the non-financial benefits gained from the projects including skills acquisition, knowledge

Table 8.6 *Assessment of livelihoods analysis*

Positive

By looking beyond cash incomes, livelihoods approaches are able to get a more nuanced view of how tourism benefits poor, rural communities

Negative as well as positive impacts are covered: this can be both for direct participants and for other local people not directly involved

Assessment is based on actual observable impacts and views of local people, not assumptions

Significance is assessed in terms of what it means to poor people, and not just financial impacts

Negative

Livelihoods approaches have generated a plethora of small-scale qualitative case studies which are difficult to aggregate and use to inform policy making

Livelihoods analysis can become formulaic, slavishly following the headings of the Sustainable Livelihoods Framework (such as outlined in DFID in 2001)

Analysis tends to be restricted to rural areas, and is rarely applied to urban or mass tourism

Livelihoods analyses have been applied to poorly conceived and commercially unsustainable community tourism projects and, through an appeal to non-financial (and sometimes almost metaphysical) benefit stream, poor projects have been justified

Which pathway, which poor?

Livelihoods analysis can include assessment of direct flows (pathway 1), and those indirect flows (pathway 2) that reach people in the local geographic area of study

It covers a range of dynamic effects, such as relating to access to natural assets, participants' capacity to influence policy and changes in other economic activities It does not cover the kind of 'big picture' dynamic impacts (on economic growth rates) of the economic tools above

The unique contribution of the livelihoods approach in this context is that it has a framework to consider non-financial effects

The focus is generally poor communities living close to tourist product

It includes poorer groups who are not able to directly earn income from tourism but are affected by it

It is unlikely to include impacts on poor people outside the destination

---

and confidence of tourism and business, gender awareness and a sense of proprietorship (Murphy and Halstead, 2003).

Others take a more critical stance to illustrate the possible disruption of livelihoods from tourism from either a social or academic vantage point (Broham, 1996; Homewood and Brockington, 1999; Scheyvens, 2002; Cernat and Gourdon, 2005; Siegel and Alwang, 2005; Solomon, 2005; Jules, 2005; Mycoo, 2006).

Livelihoods analysis can only ever provide a partial picture of pro-poor impact, but it is an important complement to conventional economic techniques because it goes beyond financial flows and interprets impact from the perspective of poor people.

Enterprise analysis

Enterprise analysis uses firm-level data from tourism businesses to assess impacts. Analysis of the impacts of specific tourism enterprises is usually undertaken to assess the extent of cash flow into local pockets, and other forms of local linkages, largely with a view to increasing them. This form of analysis

Table 8.7 *Assessment of enterprise analysis*

Positive

Based on actual firm-level data not assumptions

Unpacks details of enterprise financial flows, which can be used to calculate a range of types of impacts

Combination of quantitative and qualitative data, and firm-level discussions enable assessment of causality and context

Examines the impact of core tourist business functions (staffing and procurement) on poor people rather than just focusing on CSR expenditure

Comparison across several enterprises enables identification of key determinants of the size and nature of pro-poor flows

An invaluable complement to many other methods, including value chain mapping, livelihoods analysis and economic modeling

Negative

Difficulties of generalizing from small-scale surveys

Identifies flows and action areas at firm level, but not necessarily at destination level

Tendency to focus on the accommodation sector rather than other components of the tourism value chain

Which pathway, which poor?

Both direct and indirect financial flows (pathways 1 and 2) are likely to be measured

The method tends to focus on first round impacts, so normally does not deal with induced impacts (part of pathway 2) or dynamic effects (pathway 3)

Only people who are direct recipients of first round flows from the business are 'visible', so those who are indirectly affected are generally unwittingly excluded

It usually focuses on recipients in the vicinity of tourist destinations, though in principle could include analysis of flows to workers or suppliers from elsewhere

---

usually involves detailed interviews with, for instance, hotel owners and local entrepreneurs. Ideally, enterprise analysis and livelihood analysis complement each other, with the former quantifying what flows from the enterprise, and the latter assessing its significance in people's lives.

Initially, enterprise analysis focused on one or a few, already pro-poor, businesses in very specific destinations (Elliot and Mwangi, 1998; Spenceley, 2001; Halstead, 2003; Bramman and Fundación Acción Amazonia, 2001). It has been applied to enterprises of varying size, from community run ventures, usually as a contribution to livelihoods analysis (Murphy, 2003; Dixey, 2005), to formal sector corporate ventures, in order to assess their local linkages or corporate social responsibility approach (McNab, 2005; Ashley and Haysom, 2006; Spenceley, 2005).

These micro-analyses are able to deal with issues of benefit distribution among the poor, causality, non-financial benefit flows and the role of human agency in influencing the configuration of benefit flows in the local area. More diffuse secondary effects of tourist activity, dynamic effects on growth of the local or national economy, and in particular those impacting beyond the vicinity of the tourist product are not captured by this kind of analysis. The focus of many of these analyses on small-scale lodges has made generalizations regarding mainstream tourism problematic.

There are a small number of examples where enterprise analysis has been aggregated across several enterprises in order to build a picture of typical flows, benchmarks and explanatory factors. This was done to analyse pro-poor financial flows in African Safari Lodges (Massyn and Koch, 2004a, 2004b) and Caribbean resorts (Lengefeld and Beyer, 2006), and to assess the barriers confronting tourism enterprises in South Africa (Kirsten and Rogerson, 2002). In other cases, the interviews or surveys are spread across all types of enterprise within one destination, such as Rogerson's (2002) assessment of the Highlands Meander, and the DCDM Consulting (2006) survey of tourism in Livingstone, both of which explore the contribution being made by tourism activities to local development. In addition to examining pro-poor flows, this approach can also address tourism's economic importance in terms of its value added and employment impacts (Sharma, 2003).

These comparative studies are useful for generating aggregate data based on the synthesis of very detailed empirical data, rather than assumptions. They are able therefore to compare and contrast between types of similar enterprise and to identify causal factors resulting in differences in their impacts, such

Table 8.8 *Assessment of local economic mapping and pro-poor VCA*

Positive
Put pro-poor flows in the context of the overall tourism economy
Highlight and explore the importance of supply chains to the poor
Take a destination focus and thus can support policy making at destination level
Enable decisions for pro-poor intervention to be based on an overview and comparative enterprise-level information, rather than assumptions that a certain type of tourism is most likely to be pro-poor
Able to use 'tried and tested' frameworks and tools from local economic development approaches
VCA can examine the tourist destination in the context of a global value chain
Studies tend to be relatively quick, market aware and policy focused
Destination-level focus facilitates interaction among stakeholders at destination level to encourage policy relevance and implementation

Negative
Approaches are still evolving and not yet standardized
Relatively more effort goes into mapping the current situation than identifying options for future enhancement of pro-poor impact
The focus on the destination means little can be said about the impact of tourism on the broader economy or impact on poor households outside the destination

Which pathway, which poor?
The focus is on pathways 1 and 2, with generally good mapping of indirect impacts (pathway 2)
Treatment of dynamic impacts (pathway 3) is often weak and sporadic
Local economic mapping generally only examines linkages in the destination, whereas pro-poor value chains will consider indirect linkages beyond this tight geographical boundary
The extent to which income to more distant poor suppliers is tracked varies

---

Phase	Step	What to do?	Why?
Phase 1: Diagnosis	Step 1	Preparation	To define the destination, type of potential target groups and assessment team/partners
	Step 2	Map the big picture: enterprises and other actors in the tourism sector, links between them, demand and supply data, and the pertinent context	To organize a chaotic reality, understand the overall system
	Step 3	Map where the poor do and don't participate	To avoid erroneous assumptions about poor actors. To take account of the less visible suppliers
	Step 4	Conduct fieldwork interviews in each node of the chain, with tourists and service providers, including current/potential poor participants	To provide data and insights for Steps 5 to 8
	Step 5	Track revenue flows and pro-poor income. Estimate how expenditure flows through the chain and how much accrues to the poor. Consider their returns and factors that enable or inhibit earnings	To follow the dollar through the chain down to the poor, and assess how returns can be increased
Phase 2: Scope and prioritize opportunities	Step 6	Identify *where* in the tourism value chain to seek change: which node or nodes?	To select areas ripe for change drawing on Steps 1 to 5. To ensure Steps 6 to 8 are focused on priority areas
	Step 7	Analyse blockages, options and partners in the nodes selected, to generate a long list of possible interventions	To think laterally and rationally in generating the range of possible projects
	Step 8	Prioritize projects on the basis of their impact and feasibility	To generate a project shortlist, comprising projects most likely to deliver impact
Phase 3: Feasibility and planning	Step 9	Project feasibility and planning	Package selected projects for funding and implementation

Figure 8.1 *Tourism value chain diagnosis*

as the structure of joint venture arrangements (Massyn and Koch, 2004a), corporate commitment to training initiatives (Lengefeld and Stewart, 2004), their championing of CSR (Spenceley, 2003), or the supply capacity of the local economy (Relly, 2004a, 2004b).

Local economic mapping and pro-poor VCA

Mapping of the local economy is a methodology adapted from local economic development to trace the flow of tourist expenditure through a destination in order to identify and assess benefit flows to the beneficiaries. The approach is based largely on primary data collection, through interviews and surveys of tourists, hoteliers and a range of other stakeholders in the tourism value chain.

VCA also focuses on the tourism value chain in the destination and supply chains and supporting institutions. However, in addition, value chain analysis seeks to understand the entire series of transactions between the source country and the tourist destination, including the activities of international tour operators and how they cooperate with local service providers. While conventional VCA is focused on competitiveness and efficiency of the sector, pro-poor VCA focuses on how the operation of the value chain impacts on poor people, particularly in terms of flows of pro-poor income.

The distinguishing feature of VCAs is that they deliver an estimate of the total flows of income coming to different poor participants in a tourism destination. They also enable disaggregated data so that different elements of the value chain can be compared. They thus differ from conventional enterprise analysis because flows from all types of enterprises are considered, and they differ from other destination-level analyses, such as SAMs, because of the disaggregation by type of poor person and type of supply chain.

Moving from VCA to value chain development, this approach can also have the explicit aim of identifying intervention areas of potential to increase pro-poor flows. Figure 8.1 explains the sequence where the analysis moves from diagnosis to identifying and prioritization of pro-poor interventions.

VCA provides a framework to assess the commercial and power relations between stakeholders which is a useful tool for analysing the barriers to entry and the means of incorporation of the resource poor in the tourism value chain. In the past, VCA over-emphasized the importance of stakeholders operating within the chain, almost to the exclusion of external stakeholders. As we implement studies in developing country destinations, issues involving the public governance of the tourism value chain continually arise – often these are the source of binding constraints on the development of pro-poor value chains.

Another important difference between pro-poor VCA and previous enterprise or livelihood-focused pro-poor analyses is that the question of shares of benefits reaching the poor does not have to be isolated from issues of growth of the overall sector. VCA has been used to answer questions both about how to increase the size of the tourism sector and also how to distribute its benefits more progressively. The logic of this approach also cautions against trying to establish an 'alternative' type of tourism that will benefit the poor – but rather to focus on the barriers preventing the poor from being beneficiaries of the mainstream tourism sector. As such, pro-poor VCA is a direct challenge to the remarkably dated view, still influential in parts of the tourism and development literature, that poverty reduction is most effectively achieved through the pursuit of equity rather than growth (Schilcher, 2007).

Simply mapping the destination economy or value chain provides a static picture. However, the application of a 'local economic development' lens to tourism transforms a static analysis into a normative exercise. This considers dynamic impacts on enterprise development, such as via clustering or skills development, or removing bottlenecks to local supplier participation. Rogerson (2005a), in a review of Livingstone, Zambia, finds strong rationale for a local economic development approach to tourism-led development. The Zambezi Sun and Royal Livingstone Hotel's US$65 million investment increased direct employment in Livingstone by 25 per cent. In addition, the hotels have created a dense network of employment opportunities in associated services, including small businesses responding to the out-sourcing of laundry, gardening, security and restaurant services. A local economic development perspective also identifies the limited local development impact on agriculture of the development of this tourist destination – as a cause of concern and a justification for an intervention to strengthen agricultural linkages.

Recent applications of local economic mapping and tourism VCA by ODI indicates that they can be insightful in very different contexts and destinations accounting for distinct types of tourists.

Mapping pro-poor participation and income in a tourism value chain or local tourism economy has been an important step forward in our understanding of poverty impacts of tourism. While the approach is still evolving and is intrinsically weak on dynamic effects, it is valuable to combine many types of enterprise analysis into one composite picture. This allows a pro-poor focus to be combined with a destination perspective, and pro-poor policy issues to be tackled in conjunction with sector growth issues, and obviates the need to make assumptions about which sectors of tourism are more pro-poor.

Developing and enhancing the tourism sector, its growth and competitiveness

Master planning

Governments need to be able to make informed decisions on whether, how and where to allocate scarce resources to develop the tourism sector, make best use of national assets and optimize benefits for poverty reduction. Many African countries have developed tourism master plans, which are often financed with concessionary funds from donors. They normally involve a team of consultants, several months of work, and considerable information gathering on market segments, visitor spending and satisfaction, and investment options.

The Tanzania tourism master plan produced by CHL Consulting (2002) is a relatively typical tourism master plan. It is based on a SWOT (strengths, weaknesses, opportunities, threats) analysis of the tourism sector. It contains a four-paragraph section on the economic significance of the sector, which

---

Box 8.1 *Missing data in master plans*

The Nigerian tourism master plan (Government of the Federal Republic of Nigeria et al, 2006) begins with the significance of the sector, but points out repeatedly and strongly that useful data are lacking.

There are signs, however, that master planning is changing. The Jordanian tourism development strategy (Hashemite Kingdom of Jordan, 2004) uses situation analysis and then VCA to assess national competitiveness in tourism over the performance of alternative destinations.

---

repeats estimates of employment and GDP contribution. But there are no other data on the impacts of different aspects of tourism or policy options. In the absence of these, the plan takes a firm policy position. It chooses to seek low-volume high-yield international tourists for whom Tanzania would be a single destination. This is to be done via developing a wider range of special interest products: activity, soft adventure, beach resort and cultural products. The weakness of the data is recognized and the master plan reports that a working group has been established to work on tourism satellite accounts.

The Gambian tourist development master plan, by contrast, has an excellent empirical basis, two detailed 2000 tourist surveys – one collected from tourists in hotels and the other from tourists departing from the international airport (Emerging Markets Group, 2005). Notwithstanding this hugely expensive data collection process, the master plan makes rather limited use of the data collected. In several cases, the master plan makes policy recommendations (supporting a move towards up-market tourists and all-inclusive resorts) that the empirical data collected during the planning process provide a basis for questioning.

Table 8.9 *Assessment of conventional master plans*

Positive
Widespread and often a good source of publicly available data
Some recent signs of more analytical and robust master planning exercises being undertaken
One of the few areas of tourism research with a well-established funding mechanism

Negative
Limited analytical consideration of poverty impacts of tourism
Inadequate treatment of inter-sector linkages
Often donor and consultancy-driven documents
Empirical basis of policy prescriptions is often unclear
Expensive and time-consuming planning documents

Which pathway, which poor?
At their worst, no focus on pathways to the poor, nor any systematic approach to linkages between tourism and the non-tourist economy

---

The master plan also fails to analyse the link between tourism and poverty in the country with the fourth lowest Human Development Index indicator in the world and a very significant tourist sector – compared with the rest of the economy. Links between tourism and the non-tourist economy are also given scant treatment. As a result of political dynamics within The Gambia and some questioning of policy proposals, a $0.5 million master plan financed by the African Development Bank and which took five years to develop has been log-jammed at draft report stage since mid-2005.

Most master plans have generated large volumes of data but with relatively little understanding about how tourism affects poverty, or even the wider economy. Information needs have not been designed in order to answer policy questions about how to enhance developmental benefits of tourism. Fortunately, as with the Jordanian example and recent work in Madagascar, there is some evidence that more rigorous analytical tools and approaches are enriching the tourism master planning process. These islands of 'best practice' are important because they could form the basis of a process of raising the quality of tourism master planning more generally through a demonstration effect.

Competitiveness analysis of the tourism value chain

Conventional VCA is a tool used in assessing competitiveness of the tourism sector (note this is different from the use of pro-poor VCA described above, to assess flows that reach down to the poor). A value chain is the series of transactions between the inputs to a production process through manufacture to distribution and sale and the eventual disposal or recycling of the product. Tourism, however, is not a product – rather, a complex set of complementary tourist services. Because services cannot be stored, production and consumption are usually simultaneous and most take place at a specific geographical location – the tourist destination. Assessment of the value chain looks at all operations, from pre-departure planning to post-trip return.

VCA emphasizes the need to look at transactions at all points across the value chain, from producer to consumer, and thus has a strong focus on inter-sector linkages. Although focused on competitiveness, not impact, they usually do include an assessment of returns to different stakeholders or parts of the chain. They have recently started to take into account more sociological issues of economic power and governance.

The noticeable change in analysis is the recognition of the importance, and measurement of the efficiency and competitiveness, of firms in the entire value chain. For instance, a VCA assessing competitiveness constraints in Mozambique identified factors such as the operation of border crossings as a major constraint on several tourist value chains in the country (FIAS, 2006). Although it is still too early to determine the relative merits of this new approach, the success of other industry sectors such as manufacturing, horticulture and telecoms in developing countries has been facilitated by this kind of detailed analysis.

Table 8.10 *Assessment of VCA*

Positives
Disaggregation of different market segments facilitates policy planning
Effectively identifies bottlenecks – whether within the tourism sector or not – that are impairing the efficiency of the whole value chain
Focuses on cooperation and inter-dependence between different firms within the value chain
Examines the whole chain of transactions between the tourist source market and the destination

Negatives
VCA tends to examine only the first round effects with little disaggregation of supply chains, so reveals little about the participation of the poor in supply chains
Linkages between tourism and the rest of the economy are not a particular focus

Which pathway, which poor?
Conventional VCA has no focus on pathways, but is likely to generate data that are useful for understanding pathway 2
If extended to the level of workers and suppliers, it could provide information on pathway 1

VCA is a useful approach to structure questions relating to how the value generated by tourism is distributed throughout the value chain, how the product is experienced by customers, the nature of inter-dependence between players in the chain, and which are the bottlenecks that are constraining the overall sector.

Analysis of competitive advantage, or bottlenecks to competitiveness, is an area of growing attention, and VCA is not the only tool. Some studies, such as a Diagnostic Trade Integration Study for Tanzania (Sharma, 2005) and a competitiveness study for Rwanda (OTF Group, 2006), assess a range of export sectors in terms of their markets, returns, international competitiveness and potential. It is from this analysis that tourism emerges as a priority.

Conventional VCA in order to enhance competitiveness does not, in itself, inform pro-poor policy, but is a useful complement as it provides the context in which the overall sector needs to develop.

Across the methods

All the methods are partial in their coverage of the impact that tourism has on poverty – although the degree of partiality varies. Several approaches are useful for shedding light on two of the three pathways, and some methods generate an input to other more complex analytical techniques. Because none of the methods examined above provide answers for all three pathways, however, none should be used in isolation. There is no magic methodological tool and our best chance of understanding reality is to adopt a multi-methods approach.

Given this, there is remarkably little work in the literature that combines methods from different research approaches (e.g. livelihoods analysis plus economic modelling), or that compares the utility of different methods (e.g. findings of VCA and I–O models concerning inter-sectoral linkages). Authors tend to assume their chosen approach is the obvious one, with little reference to alternatives, and little attempt to see what value could be added by adopting a comparative approach.

As Ghali (1976) pointed out three decades ago, measuring the total contribution of tourism to output is not the same as measuring its contribution to welfare. Asking 'how much did tourism contribute?' is interesting, but does not necessarily address the difficult question of 'was it worth it?' None of the methods reviewed here adequately take account of the costs of achieving the tourism that caused the measured impact, nor of the non-financial aspects of welfare.

These findings lead us to conclude that traditional measures of the impact of tourism do not provide a complete insight into the magnitude of impacts on the poor. They do not enable stakeholders to unequivocally relate tourism trends to all changes in poverty. There is no shortage of research methods available to examine different aspects of how tourism impacts on poverty. Each has strengths and weaknesses and none justifies an exclusive focus. What we need is a bit of renaissance thinking. Researchers should be driven more by the need to get as close as possible to the right answer rather than being wedded to asking the question in a particular way. Our goal is to better understand the links between tourism and poverty with the primary goal of enhancing the livelihoods of the poor. Applying whatever research methods are most appropriate for each given situation is a means to this primary goal, not an end in itself.

We are particularly impressed by the promise of a combination of pro-poor VCA and CGE modelling approaches to provide a broad understanding of linkages between tourism and the rest of the economy together with a detailed knowledge of the operation of specific destinations.

It is important to appreciate the advantages of different methods including the capacity of:

- pro-poor VCA to assess pro-poor impacts across a destination, and between different types of tourism service;
- VCA and I–O models to assess inter-sectoral linkages;
- SAMs to bring together social and economic variables and disaggregate findings between different groups of household;
- CGE modelling to assess longer-term economic changes, and to model policy scenarios;
- Livelihoods analysis to capture non-financial and dynamic impacts, and to put assessment in terms of the priorities of the poor themselves;
- Enterprise and livelihoods analysis to explore context and causality;
- Regression analysis to seek to understand relationships between variables that might have general application, rather than be seduced by geographic exceptionalism.

Note

1 For example, estimates of multipliers for Tanzania have existed for several years (Kweka et al, 2001, 2003; Kweka, 2004) but are not mentioned in tourism planning documents. When multiplier estimates from different countries and authors are quoted and collated, it tends to be without discussion of their different methodologies and definitions, yet as Lejárraga and Walkenhorst (2006) point out, these differences make them incomparable.

9

A Different Perspective on Tourism and Poverty

We started this book stating the need to figuratively 'climb a tree' for an aerial view of how tourism affects the lives of poor people. Despite a plethora of case studies, academic articles and plans, research has been so piecemeal that we are only now beginning to pull the pieces together robustly enough to answer this basic question. This book is an attempt to synthesize evidence from different destinations, methods and types of impact in order to build a more comprehensive picture. This we have done, by grouping the multiple impacts into three main pathways, and then exploring the evidence for impacts within each pathway.

Another point of departure for this book was seeking to move beyond the sterile dichotomy of views on the role of tourism in development. A chasm lies between tourism protagonists and tourism critics. The protagonists extol the size and virtues of the tourism sector, invest in satellite accounting to 'prove' its scale and counteract its invisibility to governments, or argue that tourism is inherently pro-poor because of its employment structure or linkages with other sectors. The critics maintain that the bulk of tourism spending 'leaks' out of the economy, leaving community disruption rather than prosperity in its wake. The evidence we have compiled here challenges both positions. Tourism cannot simply be assumed to be good for development and the poor, but many of the claims of the 'leakage' of benefits generated by tourism at destinations are ludicrously weak.

The third and final driver for this book was the growing need of policy makers for evidence to inform their decisions on investment in poverty reduction and growth, including pro-poor growth and low-carbon growth. They face trade-offs in deciding which sectors to invest in, how to attract foreign or domestic investment, how far to liberalize trade, and how to ensure that growth helps them achieve the MDGs. As companies and governments increasingly quantify the carbon footprint of any activity, the need to be clear on the development value of any sector, but particularly tourism, will only increase. Hard choices will need to be made about which carbon-emitting activities are most 'worthwhile', and such choices require evidence. So, while synthesizing the patchy evidence base to date, we have also highlighted directions for future research methods, so that a more robust and useful evidence base can be established over time.

Having climbed the metaphorical tree, the landscape in view contains scattered jigsaw pieces, some of which fit together, some contradict, and others are simply missing. Despite the gaps, eight important points emerge from this viewpoint, summarized below.

All three pathways by which tourism impacts on poverty need consideration

To understand why tourism sometimes 'works' – as a driver of growth that benefits the poor – and sometimes does not, requires an understanding of the range of linkages between tourism and the local economy and poor people within it. There are many different ways in which tourism affects poor people. Some of these linkages are entirely obvious and others are much less so – indeed several of the dynamic linkages between tourism and the poor were a revelation to us. Not surprisingly, each piece of research has a different focus. Whether it is the impact of coastal development on fishermen, or the impact of tourism growth on the exchange rate and export competitiveness, each piece is useful. But it is important that researchers and policy makers know what falls outside the scope of any piece of research, and not just what is included.

Policy makers need the big picture of myriad diverse impacts to consider and, to achieve this, they need a way to get a handle on them. The conceptual framework we developed in Chapter 2 seeks to encompass and categorize the many different ways that tourism can affect the resource poor. While any categorization can be debated, we find that looking at the many positive and negative impacts of tourism on the poor as transmitted via the three main pathways is helpful. We should stress that this framework is not just useful in the corridors of academia. Our job is to apply this framework in some of the most peripheral and poorest tourist destinations in the world and to use the analysis as a basis for practical advice to public and private sector decision makers. The framework has been tested in the real world and it works.

Pathway 1: Direct effects of tourism on the poor
These include both labour income and other forms of earnings from the tourist sector. They also include direct effects of tourism on the poor even if they are non-financial livelihood changes.

Pathway 2: Secondary effects of tourism on the poor
This includes indirect earnings (and non-financial livelihood impacts) from non-tourism sectors that arise from tourist activity. Also included are induced effects from tourism workers who re-spend their earnings in the local economy.

Pathway 3: Dynamic effects on the economy and patterns of growth

This includes longer-term effects whether experienced in the macro-economy, or limited to the local economy at the destination. Some environmental impacts, such as the erosion of natural assets from tourist developments can be conceived as dynamic effects.

The pathways were outlined in more detail in Chapters 4 to 7, and are summarized again in Figure 9.1.

The three pathways are not water-tight categories and precise boundaries can always be contested. However, this conceptual framework has proved useful in organizing our thoughts and understanding why different studies have looked at tourism in such contrasting ways. It also explains why almost all studies of the links between tourism and poverty have been missing an important part of the picture. Most look at just one pathway: perhaps direct community earnings, food chain linkages or dynamic impacts on growth. Some look at two pathways: direct and indirect earnings, or short-term and long-term livelihood change. Virtually no research is grounded in all three, although some recent innovative equilibrium modelling work does assess impacts on the economy through all three pathways.

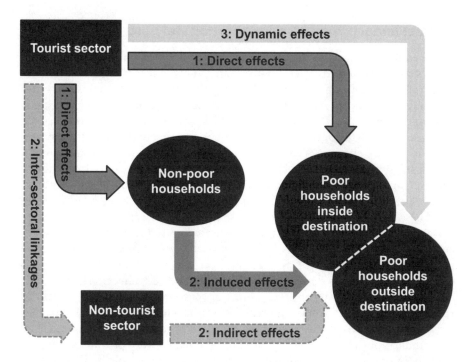

Figure 9.1 *Three pathways of benefits to the poor from tourism*

Direct impacts are the most evident though not always the most significant

Tourism creates jobs, particularly for women and low-skilled workers. Data presented in Chapter 4 reinforce the evidence base that tourism is labour-intensive relative to other non-agricultural sectors. But as Chapter 3 illustrates, direct earnings of the poor from employment in tourism are not always the largest pro-poor financial flow. The scale of direct earnings varies enormously, depending on labour market conditions and the share of employment accruing to local people. For countries without a strong entrepreneurial environment and/or with unskilled and semi-skilled wages set at high levels (due to minimum wage regulations or a tightening labour market), the wages paid to non-management staff are a very important element of the flow of resources from tourism to the poor. Elsewhere, direct wages generate a smaller share of the benefits of tourism. The poor can also benefit from tourism by working in small tourist businesses. These opportunities are sometimes more accessible than formal sector jobs. Critical to the scale of informal sector tourist opportunities is the extent of out-of-pocket expenditure by tourists. Non-wage income varies widely. In a few cases, collective income from joint ventures or philanthropic donations is large enough to alter the overall impact of tourism on flows to the poor, but these cases are few.

Indirect impacts may be disproportionately pro-poor

Poor people can earn substantial income indirectly from tourism via the food, construction sector and other supply chains. This makes the gaps in past research all the more unfortunate. On the one hand, supply chains were too often neglected in early pro-poor tourism studies, while on the other, economic assessment and satellite accounts invested heavily in tracking inter-sectoral linkages, but with little attention to the benefit accruing to the poor. Fortunately this has already changed. Pro-poor value chain analyses now illustrate that a significant share of pro-poor income in a destination can come from supply chains. Conversely, improved economic models can incorporate distributional effects, showing the pro-poor impact of linkages.

These data provide some evidence that indirect effects are not only large but also disproportionately pro-poor, compared with direct effects. Multiplier analyses suggest that, in terms of economic contribution, indirect effects are generally 60–80 per cent of the size of direct effects. Importantly though, as a share of the benefits flowing to poor people, indirect effects are often (but not always) more significant than direct effects. Indirect effects also tend to reach large numbers of poor households (albeit with possibly small earnings per household) and can have geographical reach beyond the destination. Given these indications that they are a particularly effective way of transmitting the benefits of tourism to very large numbers of very poor people, indirect effects should be a focus of attention for policy makers.

Dynamic impacts are critical but poorly understood

It is possible that most of the poverty-mitigating effects from tourism development in the long run are derived from dynamic effects (pathway 3). Tourism growth can facilitate infrastructure development and human resource development, and the raising of taxes to finance these investments. International tourism brings global consumers within the national borders of poor and peripheral countries. This can expose indigenous entrepreneurs to international tastes, which can support export diversification.

There is also sufficient evidence of mechanisms by which tourism can damage the livelihoods of the poor to be cautious of the assumption that tourism development inevitably benefits them. Under certain circumstances, rapid tourism growth may be harmful for large numbers of vulnerable households, for example, by hindering the competitiveness of smallholder agricultural exporters through exchange rate appreciation. Evidence of tourism impacting upon prices, wages, the external value of the currency and growth itself is mixed. Tourism development often appears to result in faster, but more volatile, growth. So even though tourism is a significant part of the economy of many poor countries, researchers cannot simply conclude that, because tourism is big, it must be developmentally benign. In fact, the size and buoyant growth of tourism can – under specific circumstances – create the conditions that actually harm the welfare of other poor people.

It is quite conceivable that in some cases one particularly strong dynamic impact – whether positive or negative – may override the significance of all other flows: for example, if exchange rate appreciation damages the competitiveness of the agricultural sector, or if a new road brings a remote area into the national economy. However, the evidence on dynamic impacts is patchy, and there has been no attempt so far to weigh dynamic impacts against the other more tangible impacts on the poor. What is clear is that researchers and policy makers need to bring them into the debate. While governments need to base decisions on short-term impacts on their constituents lives, they also need to know how they affect long-term objectives for economic transformation.

The overall share of tourism spending reaching the poor is higher than critics claim

A question this book has wrestled with is whether tourism expansion is a 'good bet' for growth that benefits the resource poor. Based on recent detailed research, the answer appears to be that tourism can be an effective transmission mechanism for resource flows from affluent tourists to the resource poor. Most destinations fall into the range of 10–30 per cent of in-country tourist spending accruing to poor people around that destination. This finding contrasts sharply with many of the claims that international tourism is of virtually no benefit to the hosts. What is true, however, is that the extent to which destinations and poor people within them benefit from tourism varies greatly.

Policy context matters a lot, the type of tourism matters little

There is evidence that different kinds of tourism generate different distributional impact on the host population. This evidence is remarkably patchy. What we can say with complete certainty is that many of the assumptions that have influenced public policy in this area (that eco-tourism, CBT or independent travel are inherently pro-poor and package tourism is not) simply are not substantiated.

We have found destinations where the share of tourism spending reaching the poor is only around 5 to 10 per cent of tourism spending, and these vary from gorilla tourism in Central Africa, to business tourism in Ghana and cultural tourism in Cambodia. Just because a tourism segment is based on culture or wildlife does not mean it is pro-poor. And just because it is built around business tourism or large-scale leisure resorts does not mean it is not pro-poor. These assumptions are not helpful.

Factors that help to shape impacts on poor people are more likely to be the economic, policy and cultural context, and specifics of implementation. On the supply side, it matters whether local workers have skills to fill tourism jobs, whether local enterprises have skills, access and the appropriate networks to tap into tourism, and whether the incentives influencing the formal sector encourage them to source and invest locally, or seek economies of scale and compliance with standards by relying on inputs from afar. On the demand side, value chain analyses have quantified and demonstrated a point that has long been recognized in pro-poor tourism: what tourists spend, and how much they spend it, really matters. It turns out that what tourists spend, and the structure of how those goods or services are provided, can have a huge impact on the lives of poor people.

Both the size of the sector and pro-poor shares matter

The value chain analyses have reinforced another critical point, which has included many tourism specialists. Both the scale of tourism activity and the share that reaches the poor are important to local people. Past research has been too focused on one or the other. As a result, policy makers have been lobbied to invest in pro-poor initiatives with no hope of reaching significant scale, or in major tourism growth with insufficient attention to linkages. In fact it is the combination of size and linkage strength which is important. In destinations where linkages are already strong (with pro-poor income around 25 per cent of in-country tourist spend) a focus on growth is likely to be appropriate. Where pro-poor income is way below international benchmarks – of, say, 10 per cent of spend – there is a clear argument for building linkages before investing further in expansion.

Researchers need to raise their game

Many tourism researchers need to raise their game. Despite significant investment of time and money in tourism research, many researchers do not yet have the analytical basis to provide decision makers with sufficiently robust advice on tourism policy. Although it is clear that no single research method in isolation is adequate, tourism researchers are rarely honest about the gaps in their own chosen methods and lack experience of applying multi-method approaches, which would fill the gaps. Our collective end of term report should read 'could try harder'.

Our discussion of direct and indirect effects showed that the micro studies are usually based on 'real' empirical data, but can rarely be generalized to a level to be useful in policy terms. Also, the mathematical analysis and modelling was elaborate but often omitted to provide answers on issues, like causality and distributional impact, on which policy makers focus. Ironically, the traditional master plan has been unable to inform debates about either inter-sector linkages or pro-poor impact.

But there is good news too. There is some evidence of a convergence amongst the different research methods reviewed. This convergence should be welcomed, along with the (largely implicit) recognition that no single research method is able to assess all the diverse linkages between tourism and the host with equal effect.

Figure 9.2 illustrates these positive shifts in tourism research. As evidence of the pro-poor impact of secondary linkages becomes clearer, pro-poor tourism studies are broadening the previous focus beyond direct impacts. Meanwhile, the more quantitative approaches, including VCA, some CGE models and

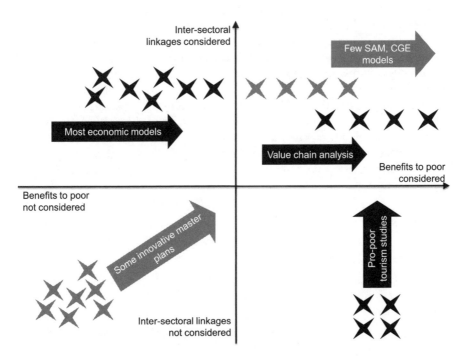

Figure 9.2 *Towards a convergence of research methods*

SAMs are realizing their potential for a much stronger focus on distributional issues. There are some hopeful signs that some tourism master plans are developing analyses that look more seriously at tourism within the macro-economy and the contribution that tourism can make to poverty reduction.

In conclusion, a nuanced reality

In international tourism, we have a very large industry comprised of pre-dominantly affluent people with a striking – and increasing – predilection for visiting developing countries. The bulk of this traffic is to middle-income destinations, but a significant share is to some of the smallest, poorest and most peripherally located countries. Tourism is now unquestionably an important sector of the economy for many low-income countries with limited alternative development options. It fits with the common aim of developing a service sector to reduce reliance on exports of commodities and other goods. And it now comprises an important share of national income – particularly when linkages to the non-tourism sector are taken into account – and a large share of total exports. The share of these gains that reach the poor, directly or indirectly, can be remarkably high, though this is not always so. A significant recent trend, amongst mainstream out-bound tour operators in parts of Europe, is that – for a whole range of statutory, marketing and ethical reasons – there is a commercial interest in improving the destination impacts of tourism.

Tourism is not a panacea for poverty reduction in the developing world. However, in some places tourism can play an important part in the battle against poverty. Whatever the strength of current links between tourism and poverty, our research has revealed that simple and practical steps can be implemented to enhance these links through a diversity of public, private and community actions. An approach is emerging to help identify the interventions most likely to have the largest pro-poor impact in the tourism value chain. As researchers, practitioners, business people and policy makers find ways to measure these pro-poor flows better, demonstrating on-the-ground success will be more plausible. This will encourage the development of a broad coalition of government, private sector, community and development sector interests that see tourism less as part of a development problem and more as part of the solution.

References

Abdool, A. and Carey, B. (2004) 'Making all-inclusives more inclusive: A research project on the economic impact of the all-inclusive hotel sector in Tobago for the Travel Foundation', www.thetravelfoundation.org.uk/assets/files/get_involved/learn_more/further_research/4a.%20Making%20all%20inclusives%20more%20all%20inclusive,%20full%20report.doc, accessed 15 June 2009

Adams, P. D. and Parmenter, B. R. (1995) 'An applied general equilibrium analysis of the economic effects of tourism in a quite small, quite open economy', *Applied Economics*, vol 27, no 10, pp985–994

Algieri, B. (2006) 'International tourism specialisation of small countries', *International Journal of Tourism Research*, vol 8, pp1–12

Archer, B. (1984) 'Economic impact: Misleading multiplier', *Annals of Tourism Research*, vol 11, no 3, pp517–518

Archer, B. and Fletcher, J. (1996) 'The economic impact of tourism in the Seychelles', *Annals of Tourism Research*, vol 23, no 1, pp32–47

Ashley, C. (2000) 'The impacts of tourism on rural livelihoods: Namibia's experience', ODI Working Paper 128, ODI, London

Ashley, C. (2005) 'Facilitating pro-poor tourism with the private sector. Lessons learned from pro-poor tourism pilots in southern Africa', ODI Working Paper 257, ODI, London

Ashley, C. (2006a) 'Participation by the poor in Luang Prabang tourism economy: Current earnings and opportunities for expansion', report prepared for SNV, ODI, London

Ashley, C. (2006b) 'How can governments boost the local economic impacts of tourism? Options and tools', toolkit prepared for SNV, ODI, London

Ashley, C. and Haysom, G. (2006) 'From philanthropy to a different way of doing business: Strategies and challenges in integrating pro-poor approaches into tourism business', *Development Southern Africa*, vol 23, no 2, pp265–280

Ashley, C. and Jones, B. (2001) 'Joint ventures between communities and tourism investors: Experience in southern Africa', *International Journal of Tourism Research*, vol 3, no 5, pp407–423

Ashley, C. and Mitchell, J. (2006) 'Tourism business and the local economy: Increasing impact through a linkages approach', ODI Briefing Paper, March, ODI, London

Ashley, C., Roe, D. and Goodwin, H. (2001) 'Pro-poor tourism strategies: Making tourism work for the poor: A review of experience', Pro-Poor Tourism Report 1, ICRT (International Centre for Responsible Tourism), IIED (International Institute for Environment and Development) and ODI, London

Ashley, C., Haysom, G., Poultney, C., McNab, D. and Harris, A. (2005) 'How to? Tips and tools for South African tourism companies on local procurement, products and partnerships', Tourism Business Council of South Africa, Republic of South Africa Department of Environment and Tourism, and Republic of South Africa Department of Trade and Industry, Pretoria

Aylward, B. and Lutz, E. (2003) *Nature Tourism, Conservation, and Development in Kwazulu-Natal, South Africa*, World Bank, Washington, DC

Bah, A. and Goodwin, H. (2003) 'Improving access for the informal sector to tourism in The Gambia'. Pro-Poor Tourism Working Paper 15, ICRT, IIED and ODI, London

Bandyopadhyay, S., Shyamsundar, P., Wang, L. and Humavindu, M. N. (2004) 'Do households gain from community-based natural resource management? An evaluation of community conservancies in Namibia', World Bank Policy Research Working Paper 3337, World Bank, Washington, DC

Barnes, J., MacGregor, J. and Weaver, C. (2001) 'Economic analysis of community wildlife use initiatives in Namibia'. Directorate of Environmental Affairs Research Discussion Paper 42, Government of Namibia Ministry of Environment and Tourism, Windhoek, Namibia

Becken, S. and Butcher, G. (2004) 'Economic yield associated with different types of tourists – a pilot analysis', www.landcareresearch.co.nz/research/sustainablesoc/tourism/documents/economic_yield_analysis.pdf, accessed 15 June 2009

Benavides, D. D. and Perez-Ducy, E. (2001) 'Tourism in the least developed countries', paper prepared for the 3rd UN Conference on the Least Developed Countries, 26–29 March, Maspalomas, Gran Canaria, Spain

Bennett, O. et al (1999) 'Sustainable tourism and poverty elimination study'. A report to the Department for International Development, April 1999, Deloitte and Touche, IIED and ODI, London, www.propoortourism.org.uk/dfid_report.pdf

Bigsten, A. and Shimeles, A. (2004) 'Prospects for 'pro-poor' growth in Africa', World Institute for Development Economics Research Paper 2004/42, Helsinki, Finland

Blake, A., Arbache, J. S., Sinclair, M. T. and Teles, V. (2008) 'Tourism and poverty relief', *Annals of Tourism Research*, vol 35, no 1, pp107–126

Bolwell, D. and Weinz, W. (2008) 'Reducing poverty through tourism', International Labour Organisation Sectoral Activities Programme Working Paper 266, Geneva

Bond, I. (2001) 'CAMPFIRE and the incentives for institutional change', in Hulme, D. and M. W. Murphree (eds.) *African Wildlife and Livelihoods: The Promise and Performance of Community Conservation*, James Currey, Oxford, UK

Boonzaaier, W. (2002) 'Joint venture decision making framework for community-based natural resource management areas', WWF LIFE Program, Namibia

Bowen, R. L., Cox, L. J. and Fox, M. (1991) 'The interface between tourism and agriculture', *Journal of Tourism Studies*, vol 2, pp43–54

Brændvang, A. K., Dybedal, P., Johansen, S. and Sørensen, K. (2001) 'Regional satellite accounts for tourism data: Concepts, methods and applications', paper prepared for the 41st European Congress of the European Regional Science Association, August–September, Zagreb, Croatia

Brakke, M. (2005) 'International tourism, demand, and GDP implications: A background and empirical analysis', Undergraduate Economic Review, Illinois Wesleyan University, IL

Bramman, S. and Fundación Acción Amazonia (2001) 'Practical strategies for pro-poor tourism: TROPIC Ecological Adventures – Ecuador', Pro-Poor Tourism Working Paper 6, ICRT, IIED and ODI, London

Brau, R., Lanza, A. and Pigliaru, F. (2003) 'How fast are the tourism countries growing? The cross-country evidence', report prepared for the International Conference on Tourism and Sustainable Economic Development – Macro and Micro Economic Issues, 19–20 September, Sardinia, Italy

Broham, J. (1996) 'New directions in tourism for third world development', *Annals of Tourism Research*, vol 23, pp48–70

Burgess, R. and Venables, J. A. (2004) 'Towards a microeconomics of growth', World Bank Policy Research Working Paper 3257, World Bank, Washington, DC

Cernat, L. and Gourdon, J. (2005) 'Is the concept of sustainable tourism sustainable? Developing the Sustainable Tourism Benchmarking Tool', http://mpra.ub.uni-muenchen.de/4178/, accessed 4 June 2009

Chao, C., Hazari, B. R., Laffargue, J., Sgro, P. and Yu, E. S. H. (2006) 'Tourism, Dutch disease and welfare in an open dynamic economy', *Japanese Economic Review*, vol 57, no 4, pp501–515

Chikosi, C., Christie, I., Habyarimana, J., Iarossi, G., Klapper, L., Nthara, K., Shah, M. and Tanzillo, G. (2006) 'Malawi investment climate assessment', Africa Private Sector Group, World Bank, Washington, DC

CHL Consulting (2002) 'Integrated tourism master plan for Tanzania: Summary and action plan update – Final report', The United Republic of Tanzania Ministry of Natural Resources and Tourism, Dar es Salaam

Chok, S. and Macbeth, J. (2007) 'Tourism as a tool for poverty alleviation: A critical analysis of pro-poor tourism and implications for sustainability', *Current Issues in Tourism*, vol 10, no 2–3, pp144–165

Choy, D. J. L. (1995) 'The quality of tourism employment', *Tourism Management*, vol 16, no 2, pp129–137

Christie, I. (2006) 'Institutions for managing tourism growth: An overview', unpublished paper, Foreign Investment Advisory Service, Washington, DC

Christie, I. and Crompton, D. (2001) 'Tourism in Africa', Africa Region Working Paper Series 12, World Bank, Washington, DC

Christie, I. and Crompton, D. (2003) 'Republic of Madagascar: Tourism sector study'. Africa Region Working Paper Series 63, World Bank, Washington, DC

Clancy, M. (2001) 'Mexican tourism: Export growth and structural change since 1970', *Latin American Research Review*, vol 36, no 1, pp128–150

Clauzel, S. (2005) 'Community development through tourism: Feasibility and demonstrativeness – Lessons learned from the Saint Lucia Heritage Tourism Programme', Saint Lucia Heritage Tourism Programme, Castries, Saint Lucia

Coles, C. and Mitchell, J. (2009) 'Pro-poor analysis of the business and conference value chain in Accra', report prepared for SNV, ODI, London

Copeland, B. R. (1991) 'Tourism, welfare and de-industrialization in a small open economy', *Economica*, vol 58, no 232, pp515–529

Crompton, E. and Christie, I. (2003) 'Senegal tourism sector study', African Region Working Paper Series 46, World Bank, Washington, DC

DCDM Consulting (2006) 'Livingstone tourism survey', Government of Zambia Ministry of Tourism, Environment and Natural Resources, Lusaka, Zambia

de Kadt, E. (1979) *Tourism – Passport to Development*, Oxford University Press, Oxford, UK

DEAT (2005) 'Tourism BEE Charter and Scorecard', Republic of South Africa Department of Environmental Affairs and Tourism, Johannesburg

DFID (1999) 'Tourism and policy elimination: Untapped potential – Report summary', Department for International Development, London

DFID (2001) 'Sustainable Livelihoods Guidance Sheet', Department for International Development, London

Diamond, J. (1977) 'Tourism's role in economic development: The case reexamined', *Economic Development and Cultural Change*, vol 25, no 3, pp539–553

Diggle, R. (2003) 'A business assessment of community-based tourism in Caprivi', MSc dissertation, University of Greenwich, London

Dixey, L. (2005) 'Inventory and analysis of community based tourism in Zambia', USAID Production, Finance and Technology' (PROFIT) Program, Lusaka, Zambia

Dwyer, L. (2005) 'Economic measures of tourism yield: Implications for destination marketing', University of New South Wales, Sydney

Dwyer, L., Forsyth, P., Madden, J. and Spurr, R. (2000) 'Economic impacts of inbound tourism under different assumptions regarding the macroeconomy', *Current Issues in Tourism*, vol 3, no 4, pp325–363

Elliot, J. (1998) 'The Isivuno model – Rocktail Bay and Banzi Safari Lodges. A case study in community-based tourism enterprise development from KwaZulu Natal', African Wildlife Foundation Discussion Paper CEC-DP-5, Nairobi, Kenya

Elliot, J. and Mwangi, M. M. (1998) 'Developing wildlife tourism in Laikipia, Kenya – Who benefits?', African Wildlife Foundation Discussion Paper CEC-DP-3, Nairobi, Kenya

Emerging Markets Group (2005) 'The Gambia Tourism Development Master Plan', Gambian Department of State for Tourism and Culture, Banjul, Gambia and the African Development Bank, Tunis-Belvedère, Tunisia

Encontre, P. (2001) 'Tourism development and the perspective of graduation from the LCD category', in WTO (eds) *Tourism in the Least Developed Countries*, WTO, Madrid

Ennew, C. (2003) 'Understanding the economic impact of tourism', paper prepared for 18th Som Nath Chib Memorial Lecture, 14 February, University of Nottingham, UK

Epler-Wood, M. (2004) 'A triple bottom line framework for sustainable tourism development for international donors: Defining indicators for conservation, community and local enterprise development', Epler-Wood International, Burlington, VT

Eugenio-Martín, J. L., Morales, N. M. and Scarpa, R. (2004) 'Tourism and economic growth in Latin American countries: A panel data approach', Fondazione Eni Enrico Mattei Research Paper 26.2004

European Commission (2003) 'Support to the Wild Coast Spatial Development Initiative Pilot Programme: Mid-term review report – Project SA/99/73200/019', Republic of South Africa Department of Environmental Affairs and Tourism, Pretoria, South Africa

Fan, T. and Oosterhaven, J. (2005) 'The impact of international tourism on the Chinese economy', paper prepared for the 15th International Input–Output Conference, June, Beijing

FIAS (Foreign Investment Advisory Service) (2006) *The Tourism Sector in Mozambique: A Value Chain Analysis*, IFC and World Bank, Washington, DC

Fletcher, J. (1989) 'Input-output analysis and tourism impact studies', *Annals of Tourism Research*, vol 16, no 4, pp514–529

Frechtling, D. C. (1999) 'The tourism satellite account: Foundations, progress and issues', *Tourism Management*, vol 20, pp163–170

Fries, R., Correa, M., Pool, D. and Rodriguez, A. (2006) *Nature-Oriented Tourism in Ecuador: An Assessment Applying the Value Chain and Nature, Wealth and Power Frameworks*, United States Agency for International Development, Washington, DC

FTO (2006) *Supplier Sustainability Handbook*, Federation of Tour Operators, London

Gerosa, V. (2003) 'Pro-poor growth strategies in Africa – Tourism: A viable option for pro-poor growth in Africa?' paper prepared for the Economic Commission for Africa Expert Group Meeting, 23–24 June, Kampala, Uganda

Ghali, M. A. (1976) 'Tourism and economic growth: An empirical study', *Economic Development and Cultural Change*, vol 24, no 3, pp527–538

Goodwin, H. (2006a) 'Measuring and reporting the impact of tourism on poverty', paper prepared for Cutting Edge Research in Tourism – New Directions, Challenges and Applications, 6–9 June, School of Management, University of Surrey, UK

Goodwin, H. (2006b) 'The poverty angle of sun, sea and sand – Maximising tourism's contribution', paper prepared for the UNCTAD/WTO International Trade Centre Executive Forum Conference, September, Berlin

Goodwin, H. (2006c) 'Community-based tourism: Failing to deliver?' *id21 Insights*, 62, Institute of Development Studies, University of Sussex, UK

Government of the Federal Republic of Nigeria, UNWTO, UNDP and Tourism Development International (2006) 'Nigeria Tourism Development Master Plan: Institutional capacity strengthening to the tourism sector in Nigeria', UNDP, Abuja, Nigeria

Grinspun, A. (2004) 'Pro-poor growth: Finding the Holy Grail', UNDP International Poverty Centre for Inclusive Growth One Pager 6, Brasilia

Gujadhur, T. (2001) 'Joint venture options for communities and safari operators in Botswana', CBNRM Support Programme Occasional Paper 6, Gaborone, Botswana

Hainsworth, D. (2006) 'Sustainable cultural tourism development and local communities country presentation: The case of Kazan hamlet, Thua Then Hue province, Vietnam', paper prepared for the International Conference on Cultural Tourism and Local Communities, 8–10 February, Yogyakarta, Indonesia

Halstead, L. (2003) 'Making community-based tourism work: An assessment of factors contributing to successful community-owned tourism development in Caprivi, Namibia', Directorate of Environmental Affairs Research Discussion Paper 60, Government of Namibia Ministry of Environment and Tourism, Namibia

Hampton, M. (1999) 'Backpacker tourism and economic development', *Annals of Tourism Research*, vol 25, no 3, pp639–660

Hampton, M. and Christensen, J. (2005) 'Exploring the relationship between tourism and offshore finance in small island economies: Lessons from Jersey', Kent Business School Working Paper Series Working Paper 76

Harrison, D. (2004) 'Working with the tourism industry: A case study from Fiji', *Social Responsibility*, vol 1, no 1–2, pp249–270

Harrison, D. and Schipani, S. (2007) 'Lao tourism and poverty alleviation: Community-based tourism and the private sector', *Current Issues in Tourism*, vol 10, no 2–3, pp194–230

Hashemite Kingdom of Jordan (2004) 'Jordan National Tourism Strategy 2004–2010', www.tourism.jo/PDFs/NTS%20Book.pdf, accessed 5 June 2009

Hatfield, R. and Malleret-King, D. (2007) 'Economic Valuation of the Virunga and Bwindi Protected Forests', submitted to International Gorilla Conservation Program, Nairobi, Kenya

Hawkins, D., Lamoureux, K. and Poon, A. (2002) *The Relationship of Tourism Development to Biodiversity Conservation and the Sustainable Use of Energy and Water Resources*, UNEP, Paris

Hemmati, M. and Koehler, N. (2000) 'Financial leakages in tourism', *Sustainable Travel and Tourism*, pp25–29

Heng, M. T. and Low, L. (1990) 'Economic impact of tourism in Singapore', *Annals of Tourism Research*, vol 17, pp246–269

Hitchins, R. and Highstead, J. (2005) *Community-based Tourism in Namibia*, ComMark Trust, Pretoria, South Africa

Homewood, K. and Brockington, D. (1999) 'Biodiversity, conservation and development in Mkomazi Game Reserve, Tanzania', *Global Ecology and Biogeography*, vol 8, pp301–313

ILO (2001) 'Human resources development, employment and globalization in the hotel, catering and tourism sector' paper prepared for the Tripartite Meeting on Human Resources Development, Employment and Globalization in the Hotel, Catering and Tourism Sector, 2–6 April, Geneva

Jamieson, W., Goodwin, H. and Edmunds, C. (2004) *Contribution of Tourism to Poverty Alleviation: Pro-poor Tourism and the Challenge of Measuring Impacts*, Transport Policy and Tourism Section, Transport and Tourism Division, UN ESCAP, Bangkok

Jenkins, C. L. (1982) 'The effects of scale in tourism projects in developing countries', *Annals of Tourism Research*, vol 9, no 2, pp229–249

Jules, S. (2005) *Sustainable Tourism in St. Lucia: A Sustainability Assessment of Trade and Liberalization in Tourism Services*, International Institute for Sustainable Development, Winnipeg, Canada

Kakwani, N. and Pernia, E. (2000) 'What is pro-poor growth?' *Asian Development Review*, vol 16, no 1, pp1–22

Kalisch, A. (2002) *Corporate Futures: Consultation on Good Practice Social Responsibility in the Tourism Industry*, Tourism Concern, London

Kirsten, M. and Rogerson, M. C. (2002) 'Tourism, business linkages and small enterprise development in South Africa', *Development Southern Africa*, vol 19, no 1, pp29–59

Kiyiapi, J., Ntiati, P. O., Mwongela, B., Hatfield, R., and Williams, D. (2005) 'A Community Business: Elerai Ranch and Conservation Area, Kenya', African Wildlife Foundation Working Paper, July 2005

Knowd, I. (2006) 'Tourism as a mechanism for farm survival', *Journal of Sustainable Tourism*, vol 14, no 1, pp24–42

Kubsa, A. (2007) 'An analysis of government incentives for increasing the local economic impacts of tourism in Ethiopia', SNV, Addis Ababa, Ethiopia

Kweka, J. (2004) 'Tourism and the economy of Tanzania: A CGE analysis', paper prepared for the CSAE Conference on Growth, Poverty reduction and Human Development in Africa, 21–22 March, Oxford, UK

Kweka, J., Morrissey, O. and Blake, A. (2001) 'Is tourism a key sector in Tanzania? Input–output analysis of income, output, employment and tax revenue', www.nottingham.ac.uk/ttri/pdf/2001_1.pdf, accessed 2 June 2009

Kweka, J., Morrissey, O. and Blake, A. (2003) 'The economic potential of tourism in Tanzania', *Journal of International Development*, vol 15, pp335–351

Lanza, A., Temple, P. and Urga, G. (2002) 'The implications of tourism specialization in the long run: An econometric analysis for 13 OECD economies', *Tourism Management*, vol 24, no 3, pp315–321

Lejárraga, I. and Walkenhorst, P. (2006) 'Of linkages and leakages: How tourism can foster economic diversification', draft report, World Bank, Washington, DC

Lengefeld, K. and Beyer, M. (2006) 'CSR beyond charity: How the core business of all-inclusive resorts contributes to poverty alleviation and local development in the Caribbean and Central America', paper prepared for BEST EN Think Tank VI Corporate Social Responsibility for Sustainable Tourism, 13–16 June, University of Girona, Spain

Lengefeld, K. and Stewart, R. (2004) 'All-inclusive resorts and local development. Sandals as the best practice in the Caribbean', www.propoortourism.org.uk/

WTM%20Presentations/WTM%20Sandals%20presentation.pdf, accessed 20 May 2009

Liaison Development Consultants (2006) 'Improving the beach management regulatory environment and legitimization of beach operators project', Government of Kenya Ministry of Tourism and Wildlife, Nairobi

Lin, T. and Sung, Y. (1984) 'Tourism and economic diversification in Hong Kong', *Annals of Tourism Research*, vol 11, pp231–247

LNTA (Lao National Tourism Administration) (2005) 'Mekong Tourism Development Project, Part B: Pro-poor community-based tourism component. Annual report: Provincial, village and household monitoring data', Lao National Tourism Administration, Vientiane, Laos

Mahony, K. and Van Zyl, J. (2001) 'Practical strategies for pro-poor tourism: Case studies of Makuleke and Manyeleti tourism initiatives', Pro-Poor Tourism Working Paper 2, ICRT, IIED and ODI, London

Medlik, S. (2003) *Dictionary of Travel, Tourism and Hospitality*, Butterworth-Heinemann, Oxford

Mann, S. (2006) *Ethiopia: Towards a Strategy for Pro-Poor Tourism Development*, World Bank, Washington, DC

Mann, S. (2007) *A Tourism Development Strategy for Ethiopia*, World Bank, Washington, DC

Massyn, P. and Koch, E. (2004a) 'African game lodges and rural benefit in two southern African countries', in Rogerson, C. and Visser, G. (eds) *Tourism and Development Issues in Contemporary South Africa*, Africa Institute of South Africa, Pretoria, South Africa

Massyn, P. and Koch, E. (2004b) 'The African safari lodge and sustainable rural development', draft report, MAFISA, Johannesburg

Mbaiwa, J. E. (2000) 'The impact of tourism in the Okavango Delta in north-western Botswana', paper prepared for a workshop on Climate Change, Biodiversity, Multi-Species Production Systems and Sustainable Livelihoods in the Kalahari Region, 1–13 October, Maun, Botswana

McKinley, T. (2006) 'What is poverty? Good question', UNDP International Poverty Centre for Inclusive Growth One Pager 26, Brasilia

McNab, D. (2005) 'Impacts of pro-poor tourism facilitation with South African corporates: Monitoring and evaluation report of the Pro-Poor Tourism Pilots Project', Pro-Poor Tourism Working Paper, ICRT, IIED and ODI, London

Metcalfe, S. (2005) 'Landscape conservation and land tenure in Zambia: Community trusts in the Kazunluga heartland', African Wildlife Foundation Working Papers, Lusaka, Zambia

Meyer, D. (2006) 'Caribbean tourism, local sourcing and enterprise development: Review of the literature', Pro-Poor Tourism Working Paper 18, ICRT, IIED and ODI, London

Meyer-Stamer, J. (2004) 'Regional value chain initiatives: An opportunity for the application of the PACA-Approach', Mesopartner Working Paper 6, Hamburg

Mitchell, J. (2008) 'Tourist development in Cape Verde: The policy challenge of coping with success', report prepared for UNDP, ODI, London

Mitchell, J. and Ashley, C. (2008) 'Strategic review of the export-led poverty reduction programme "Communities Benefiting from Tourism" approach', report prepared for ITC, ODI, London

Mitchell, J. and Coles, C. (2009) 'Enhancing private sector and community engagement in tourism services in Ethiopia', report prepared for the World Bank, ODI, London

Mitchell, J. and Faal, J. (2007) 'Package holiday tourism in The Gambia', *Development Southern Africa*, vol 24, no 3, pp445–464

Mitchell, J. and Faal, J. (2008) 'The Gambia tourism value chain and prospects for pro-poor tourism', ODI Working Paper 289, ODI, London

Mitchell, J. and Le Chi, P. (2007) 'Final report on participatory tourism value chain analysis in Da Nang, central Vietnam', report prepared for Mesopartner, ODI and Management Consulting Limited, London

Mitchell, J. and Shepherd, A. (2006) 'Productive strategies for poor rural households to participate successfully in global economic processes', report prepared for IDRC, ODI, London

Mitchell, J., Keane, J. and Laidlaw, J. (2009) 'Making success work for the poor: Package tourism in Northern Tanzania', report prepared for SNV, ODI, London

Mtui, E. (2007) 'Towards initiating and implementing incentives for pro-poor tourism in Tanzania', SNV, Arusha, Tanzania

Mullins, D. and Mulder, L. (2003) 'Tourism expenditures and regional economic development in KwaZulu-Natal: A social accounting matrix', in Aylward, B. and Lutz, E. (eds) *Nature Tourism, Conservation, and Development in Kwazulu-Natal, South Africa*, World Bank, Washington, DC

Mulonga, S. and Murphy, C. (2003) 'Spending the money: The experience of con-servancy benefit distribution in Namibia up to mid-2003', Directorate of Environ-mental Affairs Research Discussion Paper 63, Government of Namibia Ministry of Environment and Tourism, Windhoek, Namibia

Murphy, C. (2003) 'Community tourism in Kunene: A review of five case studies for the WILD Project', Directorate of Environmental Affairs Research Discussion Paper 64, Government of Namibia Ministry of Environment and Tourism, Windhoek, Namibia

Murphy, C. and Halstead, L. (2003) 'The person with the idea for the campsite is a hero: Institutional arrangements and livelihood change regarding community-owned tourism enterprises in Namibia', Directorate of Environmental Affairs Research Discussion Paper 61, Government of Namibia Ministry of Environment and Tourism, Windhoek, Namibia

Mycoo, M. (2006) 'Sustainable tourism using market regulation, market mechanisms and green certification: A case study of Barbados', *Journal of Sustainable Tourism*, vol 14, no 5, pp489–511

NACSO (2006) 'Namibia's communal conservancies: A review of progress and chal-lenges in 2005', Namibia Association of Community Based Natural Resource Man-agement Support Organizations, Windhoek, Namibia

Nicanor, N. (2001) 'Practical strategies for pro-poor tourism: NACOBTA the Namibian case study', Pro-Poor Tourism Working Paper 4, ICRT, IIED and ODI, London

Nowak, J. and Sahli, M. (2007) 'Costal tourism and "Dutch disease" in a small island economy', *Tourism Economics*, vol 13, no 1, pp49–65

O'Connell, C. (1995) 'East/West Caprivi Natural Resource Monitoring Project: Elephant/human conflicts – Final technical report', Government of Namibia Ministry of Environment and Tourism, Windhoek, Namibia

ODI and UNDP (2009) *Cambodia Country Competitiveness: Driving Economic Growth and Poverty Reduction*, UNDP Cambodia, Phnom Penh, Cambodia

Oh, C. (2005) 'The contribution of tourism development to economic growth in the Korean economy', *Tourism Management*, vol 26, pp39–44

Osmani, S. (2005) 'Defining pro-poor growth', UNDP International Poverty Centre for Inclusive Growth One Pager 9, Brasilia

OTF Group (2006) 'Briefing on competitiveness', Africa Private Sector Development Group, World Bank, Washington, DC

Page, S. (1999) *Tourism and Development: The Evidence from Mauritius, South Africa and Zimbabwe*, ODI, London

Pao, J. W. (2005) 'A review of economic impact analysis for tourism and its implications for Macao', Monetary Authority of Macao, Macao

Piccinini, J. (1999) 'Creating employment opportunities in the Windward Countries of the Eastern Caribbean', Working Paper 2, The Caribbean Project, Center for Latin American Studies, Georgetown University, Washington, DC

Poultney, C. and Spenceley, A. (2001) 'Practical strategies for pro-poor tourism, wilderness safaris. South Africa: Rocktail Bay and Ndumu Lodge', Pro-Poor Tourism Working Paper 1, ICRT, IIED and ODI, London

PPT Partnership (no date) 'What is pro-poor tourism?' www.propoortourism.org.uk/what_is_ppt.html, accessed 12 June 2009

PPT Partnership (2004) 'Pro-poor tourism update from the Pro-Poor Tourism Partnership', www.propoortourism.org.uk/PPTupdateMar04.pdf, accessed 12 June 2009

PPT Toolkit Task Team (2005) 'Private public partnerships in the tourism sector: Report 1. An analytical review of public private partnerships to date', Republic of South Africa National Treasury, Pretoria, South Africa

Ravallion, M. (2004) 'Defining pro-poor growth: A response to Kakwani', UNDP International Poverty Centre for Inclusive Growth One Pager 4, Brasilia

Relly, P. (2004a) 'Madikwe Game Reserve: The local impacts of wildlife tourism', in Rogerson, C. and Visser, G. (eds) *Tourism and Development Issues in Contemporary South Africa*, Africa Institute of South Africa, Pretoria, South Africa

Relly, P. (2004b) 'Employment and Investment in Madikwe Game Reserve, South Africa', University of Witwatersrand, South Africa

Republic of Namibia (2006) 'Valuing Namibia's parks? How increased investment in Namibia's protected areas will benefit the national economy and contribute to poverty reduction', Republic of Namibia Ministry of Environment and Tourism, Windhoek, Namibia

Rodenburg, E. (1980) 'The effects of scale in economic development: Tourism in Bali', *Annals of Tourism Research*, vol 7, no 2, pp177–196

Rogerson, C. (2002) 'Tourism and local economic development: The case of the Highlands Meander', *Development Southern Africa*, vol 19, no 1, pp143–167

Rogerson, C. M. (2005a) 'The emergence of tourism-led local development: The example of Livingstone, Zambia', *Africa Insight*, vol 35, no 4, pp112–120

Rogerson, C. M. (2005b) 'Unpacking tourism SMMEs in South Africa: Structure, support needs and policy response', *Development Southern Africa*, vol 22, no 5, pp623–642

Rogerson, C. M. (2007) 'Supporting small firm development in tourism: South Africa's Tourism Enterprise Programme', *Entrepreneurship and Innovation*, vol 8, no 1, pp1–9

Rozemeijer, N., Gujadhur, T., Motshubi, C., van den Berg, E. and Flyman, M. V. (2001) 'Community-based tourism in Botswana: The SNV experience in three community-tourism projects', SNV, Gaborone, Botswana

Sahli, M. and Nowak, J. (2005) 'Measuring the net benefits of tourism growth: The case of coastal and natural tourism in the MENA region', paper prepared for Proceedings of the Twelfth Economic Research Forum, 19–22 December, Cairo, Egypt

Sarmento, L. (2007) 'Mozambique: An analysis of government incentives for increasing the local economic impacts of tourism', SNV, Maputo, Mozambique

Saville, N. M. (2001) 'Practical strategies for pro-poor tourism: Case study of pro-poor tourism and SNV in Humla District, West Nepal', Pro-Poor Tourism Working Paper 3, ICRT, IIED and ODI, London

SBP (2005) 'Counting the cost of red tape for business in South Africa', Small Business Project, Johannesburg

Scheyvens, R. (2002) 'Backpacker tourism and third world development', *Annals of Tourism Research*, vol 29, no 1, pp144–164

Scheyvens, R. (2007) 'Exploring the tourism–poverty nexus', in Hall, C. M. (ed) *Pro-Poor Tourism: Who Benefits? Perspectives on Tourism and Poverty Reduction*, Channel View Publications, Bristol, UK

Schilcher, D. (2007) 'Growth versus equity: The continuum of pro-poor tourism and neoliberal governance', *Current Issues in Tourism*, vol 10, no 2–3, pp166–193

Shah, K. and Gupta, V. (1998) 'Stakeholder analysis based on desk research and developing methodology for case studies for fair trade in tourism research', Tourism Concern, Voluntary Service Overseas and University of North London, UK

Sharma, A. (2003) 'Economic impact and institutional dynamics of small hotels in Tanzania', Iowa State University, Iowa, IA

Sharma, A. (2005) 'Tanzania diagnostic trade integration study under the integrated framework concept paper', World Bank, Washington, DC

Sharma, A. and Olsen, M. D. (2005) 'Tourism satellite account: Implementation in Tanzania'; *Annals of Tourism Research*, vol 32, no 2, pp367–385

Siegel, P. and Alwang, J. (2005) 'Public investments in tourism in northeast Brazil: Does a poor-area strategy benefit the poor?' Latin America and Caribbean Region Sustainable Development Working Paper 22, World Bank, Washington, DC

Sinclair, M. T. (1991) 'The tourism industry and foreign exchange leakages in a developing country: The distribution of earnings from safari and beach tourism in Kenya', in Sinclair, M. T. and Stabler, M. J. (eds) *The Tourism Industry: An International Analysis*, CABI Publishing, Wallingford, UK

Sinclair, M. T. (1998) 'Tourism and economic development: A survey', *Journal of Development Studies*, vol 34, no 5, pp1–51

Sinclair, M. T., Blake, A. and Gooroochurn, N. (2004) 'Modelling tourism impacts on small island economies: Evidence from Cyprus, Malta and Mauritius', paper prepared for International Research Foundation for Development International World Forum on Small Island Developing States: Challenges, Prospects and International Cooperation for Sustainable Development, 10–11 January, Reduit, Mauritius

Sinclair, M. T., Gilham, J. and Blake, A. (2006) 'CGE tourism analysis and policy modelling', in Dwyer, L. and Forsyth, P. (eds) *The International Handbook on the Economics of Tourism*, Edward Elgar Publishing, Cheltenham, UK

Slob, B. and Wilde, J. (2006) 'Tourism and sustainability in Brazil: The tourism value chain in Porto de Galinhas, northeast Brazil', Center for Economic Research on Multinational Corporations (SOMO), Amsterdam

Smith, C. and Jenner, P. (1992) 'The leakage of foreign exchange earnings from tourism', *Travel and Tourism Analyst*, vol 3, pp52–66

Solomon, R. (2005) 'Tourism: A challenge for the 21st century', www.safarilands.org/index.php/tourism/more/tourism_a_challenge_for_the_21st_century, accessed 4 June 2009

Spenceley, A. (2001) 'A comparison of local community benefit systems from two nature-based tourism operations in South Africa', *Industry and Environment*, vol 24, no 3–4, pp50–53

Spenceley, A. (2003) 'Tourism, local livelihoods and the private sector in South Africa: Case studies on the growing role of the private sector in natural resources management' Sustainable Livelihoods in South Africa Research Paper 8, Institute of Development Studies, University of Sussex, UK

Spenceley, A. (2005) 'Tourism Investment in the Great Limpopo Transfrontier Conservation Area: Relating strategic visions to local activities that promote sustainable tourism development. Workshop proceedings', Transboundary Protected Areas Research Initiative, University of the Witwatersrand, South Africa

Spenceley, A. (ed.) (2008) *Responsible Tourism: Critical Issues for Conservation and Development*, Earthscan, London

SRI International (1997) 'Tourism development and backward linkages in the Dominican Republic', USAID, Santo Domingo, Dominican Republic

Subramanian, U. and Matthijs, M. (2007) 'Can sub-Saharan Africa leap into global network trade?', World Bank Policy Research Working Paper 4112, World Bank, Washington, DC

Sugiyarto, G., Blake, A. and Sinclair, M. T. (2002) 'Economic impact of tourism and globalisation in Indonesia', www.nottingham.ac.uk/ttri/pdf/2002_2.pdf, accessed 13 June 2009

Summary, R. M. (1987) 'Tourism's contribution to the economy of Kenya', *Annals of Tourism Research*, vol 14, no 4, pp531–540

Sutton, W., Larson, D. M. and Jarvis, L. S. (2004) 'A new approach for assessing the costs of living with wildlife in developing countries', Department of Agricultural and Resource Economics Working Paper 04-001, University of California Davis, CA

Teal, F. (2005) 'Trade and the rapid reduction of poverty in Africa', in ESRC (Economic and Social Research Council) and Development Studies Association (eds) *Africa after 2005: From Promises to Poverty*, ESRC, Swindon, UK

Telfer, D. J. and Wall, G. (1996) 'Linkages between tourism and food production', *Annals of Tourism Research*, vol 23, no 3, pp635–653

Telfer, D. J. and Wall, G. (2000) 'Strengthening backward economic linkages: Local food purchasing by three Indonesian hotels', *Tourism Geographies*, vol 2, no 4, pp421–447

Timothy, D. J. and Wall, G. (1997) 'Selling to tourists: Indonesian street vendors', *Annals of Tourism Research*, vol 24, no 2, pp322–340

Tohamy, S. and Swinscoe, A. (2000) 'The economic impact of tourism in Egypt', ECES (Egyptian Center for Economic Studies) Working Paper 40, ECES, Cairo

Torres, R. (2003) 'Linkages between tourism and agriculture in Mexico', *Annals of Tourism Research*, vol 30, no 3, pp546–566

Torres, R. and Momsen, J. (2005) 'Planned tourism development in Quintava Roo, Mexico: Engine for regional development or prescription for inequitable growth?' *Current Issues in Tourism*, vol 8, no 4, pp259–285

Travelwatch (2006) 'Increasing local economic benefits from the accommodation sector in the eastern Caribbean', www.thetravelfoundation.org.uk/assets/tools_training_guidelines/travelwatch/final%20report%20supplement%20ii.pdf, accessed 1 July 2007

Turpie, J., Lange, G., Martin, R., Davies, R. and Barnes, J. (2004) 'Strengthening Namibia's system of national protected area: Economic analysis and feasibility study for financing', Strengthening the Protected Area Network Project, Directorate of

Parks and Wildlife Management, Government of Namibia Ministry of Environment and Tourism, Windhoek, Namibia

UNCTAD (2007), 'FDI in tourism: The development dimension', UNCTAD Current Studies on FDI and Development 4, United Nations Conference on Trade and Development, Geneva,

UNDP (1996) *Human Development Report 1996*, Oxford University Press, New York

UNDP (1997) *Human Development Report 1997: Human Development to Eradicate Poverty*, Oxford University Press, New York

UNED-UK (United Nations Environment and Development UK Committee) (1999) 'Toolkit for Women. Gender & tourism: Women's employment and participation in tourism', www.earthsummit2002.org/toolkits/women/current/gendertourismrep.html, accessed 18 May 2009

UNEP (2005) *Forging Links Between Protected Areas and the Tourism Sector: How Tourism can Benefit Conservation*, United Nations Environment Programme, Paris, France

UNEP (2007) 'Economic impacts of tourism', www.uneptie.org/pc/tourism/sust-tourism/economic.htm, accessed 15 August 2007

UNWTO (2007) 'Increase tourism to fight poverty – New Year message from UNWTO', www.world-tourism.org/newsroom/Releases/2007/january/newyearmessage.htm, accessed 11 June 2009

Verdugo, D. (2007) 'An analysis of government incentives for increasing the local economic impacts of tourism in Rwanda', SNV, the Netherlands Development Organization, Kigali, Rwanda

Virola, R. A., Remulla, M. M., Amoro, L. H. and Say Milagros, Y. (2001) 'Measuring the contribution of tourism to the economy: The Philippine tourism satellite account', paper prepared for the 8th National Convention on Statistics, 1–2 October, Manila, Philippines

Wagner, J. E. (1997) 'Estimating the economic impacts of tourism', *Annals of Tourism Research*, vol 24, no 3, pp592–608

Wanhill, S. (2007) 'What do economists do? Their contribution to understanding tourism', paper prepared for The Economics of Tourism 6th DeHann Tourism Management Conference, 18 December, Nottingham University Business School, UK

Warner, M. (2005) 'Levers and pulleys: Extractive industries and local economic development', ODI Briefing Note 3, ODI, London

WEF (2007) *The Travel & Tourism Competitiveness Report 2007: Furthering the Process of Economic Development*, World Economic Forum, Geneva

Weru, J. (2007) 'Government incentives for boosting impacts on pro-poor tourism in Kenya', SNV, Nairobi

West, G. R. and Jackson, R. W. (2004) 'Non-linear input–output models: Practicability and potential', paper prepared for the 43rd Western Regional Science Association Meeting, 25–28 February, Maui, Hawaii

Williams, S. (1998) *Tourism Geography*, Routledge, UK

Williams, E., White, A. and Spenceley, A. (2001) 'UCOTA – The Uganda Community Tourism Association: A comparison with NACOBTA', Pro-Poor Tourism Working Paper 5, ICRT, IIED and ODI, London

World Bank (2006a) 'The Maldives: Sustaining growth & improving the investment climate', Finance and Private Sector Development Unit, South Asia Region, World Bank, Washington, DC

World Bank (2006b) *World Development Indicators 2006*, World Bank, Washington, DC

World Bank (2009) *World Development Indicators 2009*, World Bank, Washington, DC

WTO (2000) *General Guidelines for Developing the Tourism Satellite Account*, WTO, Madrid

WTO (2001) *Tourism in the Least Developed Countries*, WTO, Madrid

WTO (2002a) *Tourism: A Catalyst for Sustainable Development in Africa*, WTO, Madrid

WTO (2002b) *Tourism and Poverty Alleviation*, WTO, Madrid

WTO (2004) *Tourism and Poverty Alleviation Recommendations for Action*, WTO, Madrid

WTTC (no date) 'Tourism impact data and forecast tool', www.wttc.org/eng/Tourism_Research/Tourism_Impact_Data_and_Forecast_Tool/index.php, accessed 15 July 2007

WTTC (2002) *Corporate Social Leadership in Travel & Tourism*, World Travel and Tourism Council, London

WTTC (2006) *Namibia: The Impact of Travel & Tourism on Jobs and the Economy*, WTTC, London

WTTC and OE (Oxford Economics) (2006) *Methodology for Producing the 2006 WTTC/OE Travel & Tourism Simulated Satellite Accounts*, WTTC, London

Zhao, W. and Richie, B. (2007) 'Tourism and poverty alleviation: An integrative research framework', *Current Issues in Tourism*, vol 10, no 2–3, pp119–143

Index